Husband

2.0

By Herb Ellis

Print Edition

Copyright 2015 Herb Ellis

**Published by Herb Ellis, Soft BDSMi Publishing,
In conjunction with Createspace**

Createspace Press

North Charleston, South Carolina

Contents

Book disclaimer

by SEQ Legal

(1)   Introduction

This disclaimer governs the use of this book. [By accessing and/or using this book, you accept this disclaimer in full. / We will ask you to agree to this disclaimer before you can access the book.]

(2)   Credit

This disclaimer was created using an SEQ Legal template.

(3)   No advice

The book contains information about perspectives on male life and male sexuality. The information is not advice, and should not be treated as such.

[You must not rely on the information in the book as an alternative to legal / medical / financial / taxation / accountancy / religion advice from an appropriately qualified professional. If you have any specific questions about any legal / medical / financial / taxation / accountancy / religion matter you should consult an appropriately qualified professional.]

[If you think you may be suffering from any medical condition you should seek immediate medical attention. You should never delay seeking medical advice, disregard medical advice, or discontinue medical treatment because of information in the book.]

[You should never delay seeking legal advice, disregard legal advice, or commence or discontinue any legal action because of information in the book.]

(4)   No representations or warranties

To the maximum extent permitted by applicable law and subject to section 6 below, we exclude all representations, warranties, undertakings and guarantees relating to the book.

Without prejudice to the generality of the foregoing paragraph, we do not represent, warrant, undertake or guarantee:

that the information in the book is correct, accurate, complete or non-misleading;

that the use of the guidance in the book will lead to any particular outcome or result; or

in particular, that by using the guidance in the book you will produce any result, written, implied or suggested].

(5) Limitations and exclusions of liability

The limitations and exclusions of liability set out in this section and elsewhere in this disclaimer: are subject to section 6 below; and govern all liabilities arising under the disclaimer or in relation to the book, including liabilities arising in contract, in tort (including negligence) and for breach of statutory duty.

We will not be liable to you in respect of any losses arising out of any event or events beyond our control.

We will not be liable to you in respect of any business losses, including without limitation loss of or damage to profits, income, revenue, use, production, anticipated savings, business, contracts, commercial opportunities or goodwill.

We will not be liable to you in respect of any loss or corruption of any data, database or software.

We will not be liable to you in respect of any special, indirect or consequential loss or damage.

(6) Exceptions

This disclaimer shall: limit or exclude our liability for death or personal injury resulting from negligence; limit or exclude our liability for fraud or fraudulent misrepresentation; limit any of our liabilities in any way that is not permitted under applicable law; and exclude any of our liabilities that may not be excluded under applicable law.

(7)   Severability

If a section of this disclaimer is determined by any court or other competent authority to be unlawful and/or unenforceable, the other sections of this disclaimer continue in effect.

If any unlawful and/or unenforceable section would be lawful or enforceable if part of it were deleted, that part will be deemed to be deleted, and the rest of the section will continue in effect.

(8) Law and jurisdiction

This disclaimer will be governed by and construed in accordance with U.S. & English law, and any disputes relating to this disclaimer will be subject to the exclusive jurisdiction of the courts of England and Wales.

(9) Our details

In this disclaimer, "we" means (and "us" and "our" refer to) [Author & Seller(s)].

OR

In this disclaimer, "we" means (and "us" and "our" refer to) [Author & Seller(s)], a company registered in [U.S.A., England and Wales] under registration.

OR

In this disclaimer, "we" means (and "us" and "our" refer to) [Author & Seller(s)], a partnership established under [U.S. & English law].

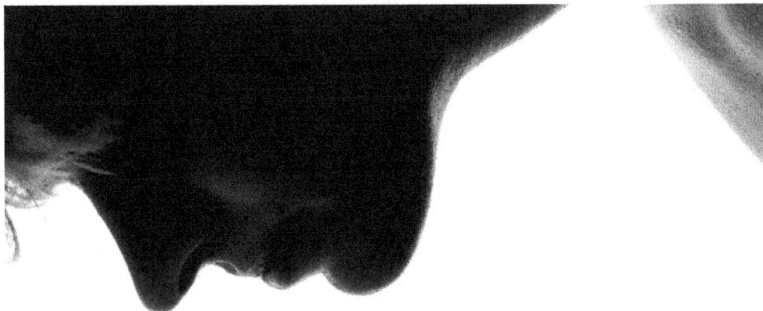

"A sister would buy this book for her brother, if he was dating her best friend"

Husband
2.0
Real Male Enhancement

Herb Ellis

Dedication

To my Mom and Dad and my sister Lynn.
"Thank You" for being here to see me actually grow up.

To my only son Xavier, grow up and be a "good" man.
If anything ever happens to me, this book
and your Bible are the only two books you will ever need.

To my daughters, Bianca and Candace,
When you are old enough to date,
if "he" has never read this book... walk away.

To my wife Katina, you are the only person that made me
want to be a better man. Thank you Katina-berry.

FOREWORD

Out of all the how-to-get-girls, how-to-seduce-women courses out there and out of all of the how-to-fix your marriage books, no one has effectively managed to produce anything for married men who want and are starving for passion and excitement in their marriage and relationships.

How does a man provide the results that will help stabilize his home with the side-effect of making him a happier and a better man?

Facts:
*Happy wife, happy life... Unhappy wife, broke husband.
*If you don't take care of your home, no one else will... Strange men may answer your wife's phone and send her text messages... But they will not take care of your home.

There are very, very serious and very, very motivated individuals fueled by Viagra and the like.... who are spending millions to learn and be trained in one thing:

"HOW TO RUN THROUGH YOUR WIFE!"

The PUA (Pick Up Artist) industry is a multi-million dollar industry and you don't really stand a chance against a jerk that has been trained to an Associate's Degree level up to a double Phd. in how to get your wife to have sex with him. I don't even want to mention You Tube and the pheromone market.

My job is to give you your edge, your tools, your mindset and your plan to do 2 things:

#1 – To significantly reduce the probability of "some-guy-running-through-your-wife".
#2 – To put you in a better position (in case that probability in #1 is near or at 100%), to either forgive her completely or to cash out and get and keep a much better woman."

How do I do my job? Without over simplifying things I go with what I know, Technical Support.

Laugh if you like, but can we agree that man is a creation? Does this creation have systems and subsystems (cardio, reproductive, endocrine, etc.)? Is there a Central Processing Unit, Arithmetic or Logic Processor, memory, short term storage and long term storage on board?

Can man, the creation, connect and communicate to similar creations for various purposes? Does man, this potentially wonderful creation, have an operating systems, excuse me... beliefs, thoughts, morals, ideas, ideals, perspectives...?

Do different men have different programs, be it talents, gifts, aptitudes, abilities and skills or the "APPLICATION" thereof?

Programs and operating systems can become corrupted and non-responsive in both man and machine. Both are prone to errors when there are problems internally or by something malicious, externally. But if you are willing to take the time, with a little effort and a very low financial investment, both can be upgraded to give a maximum ROI (Return On Investment). You do not have to throw away the computer. We do not have to throw away the man.

"(INSERT YOUR NAME HERE): a husband, a man barely alive. We can rebuild him. We have the technology. We have the capability. We can make him better than he was. Better...stronger...faster."

PREFACE

As you may have gleaned from this text, I am a very straight forward kind of guy. As much as I could write pages to describe something that I could explain in one sentence, it doesn't help you. Forcing you to wade through pages of fluff irks me. I want you to refer to the section you need, when you need it. Even the use of profanity in some sections is to get your attention in a way that fonts and formatting cannot do. I apologize if this offends anyone, but I meant what I said.

Who needs this text?

Married men, good men or men trying to be good men, in a committed relationship. Men whose real needs are not being met and are tired of waiting… Men who feel so starved for intimacy that they are "border-line psychotic". Because of inferior sex, no sex or just being tired of always being the initiator and with little or no incentive to keep trying.

Symptoms:
- Motivation and productivity suffering.
- Can't maintain focus.
- The hanging noose of an affair begins to look like a life-line.
- Starting to turn feral.

How will we accomplish our goals?

- You, creating target specific love landmines.
- Your new life plan will now include built-in incentives.
- Getting in shape.
- Making and saving money.
- Getting adequate rest.
- Accruing "coochie credits".
- Making you aware of multipliers, actions and things you can do that increase the likelihood of her being aroused.

<u>YOU</u>

For the next 30 days

Every morning when you get up and before you go to bed, recite the following:

- When it comes to my women, I will not be controlling.
- What is a priority is what gets done.
- I cannot afford to be delusional.
- I will make time to read and better myself.
- From what I have read I can solve, I can make and I can create.
- I will bring the full force of my will to bear on every task, individually.

#1 - Upgrade the BIOS

The BIOS (Basic Input and Output System) is what allows your computer to function at its most basic and initial level.

Ports, hardware, processors, the mother board... everything in the box gets detected. The optimal settings for everything to work together starts here.

Upgrading the BIOS make everything connected to the computer work better. When the manufacturer realizes something that they could have done to make the computer better i.e., work with newer technology or fix a known problem/incompatibility... they create an update for the BIOS.

Do you remember?

I listen to quite a few men. I hear them moan and groan, complain and vent. Sometimes, in the Barber Shop, sometimes in desperate phone calls. Things are wrong in their home and it is obvious, they don't know why. I do understand the frustration that they are NOT getting laid and getting affection. But that point is irrelevant, because until you deal with the "why" nothing will change.

When I ask them the question, "Do you hate your wife?" They always say, "No". Well, since they do not hate her we must deduce that they do love her. We must narrow down the point of failure. In this book, I discuss how to fix the real problem in great detail, the man.

I may not be the best writer; I may not have a degree in anything related to this subject but seriously, seriously…. I am right.

Do you remember when you were younger and getting ready for a date? In hindsight, could you honestly admit that most of the time, the activity of "getting ready for the date" was probably more exciting than the date itself? Whether you brushed your teeth until the enamel came off, forced Jheri curls or spikey hair with any chemical that you could find, endured dreds or braiding sessions lasting hours... you did things that you do NOT do now. You had to match your shoes, socks and hat, trousers and shirts even if you borrowed clothes from your friends or older brothers. You had to have jewelry, a mix tape, and the jacket... all of these things to the point of being neurotic.

This is very strange because for someone who has had our children, seen us at our best and our worst, taken vows before God to be with you and only you until they die (or you... whichever comes first)... we presently do not do 10% of the stuff that we did when we were younger to get a women or to keep one.

We have de-evolved into someone's warped perception of what a safe, sensitive proper man should be. Khaki's, ties, suits and etc. or what is required on a job, but I implore you my brothers, never to forget, as a man we descended from men who killed animals with their bare hands and worked hard for whatever else they could find to feed themselves and their families.

God gave us dominion over this earth and every creeping thing on it. On that same note, as men, we learned to make nature and the ground our bitch to grow what we wanted. But now we trust whatever the restaurants feed us and our families. But now, we buy roach spray and poison ourselves and our families, instead of reaching deep down and letting our KI (Killer Instinct), our primal nature kick in. But now, we keep mortgages, jobs and agreements with people and organizations that do not have our best interests at heart, who have already betrayed our trust before the ink was dry where we signed our name.

Husband 2.0 is the upgrade to what you already are. Once you upgrade your firmware you enable the options of being continuously and powerfully passionate and satisfied in life and in a relationship.

Your goals:
*You, having more happy moments.
*You, realizing that you can actually enjoy the time between the ultra-happy moments.
*You, maximizing your time making real and permanent positive changes in yourself.
*Your mate, discovering that the man she married is the greatest man she ever met.
*Your mate, discovering that after all these years what you are capable of being.
*Your mate, being happy she is a woman, because you are a man.

The Clark Kent/Superman Factor

Anyone who is really a Superman aficionado will agree to the following 2 statements:

Lois Lane would have gone out with Clark, if he would have made the first move.
Lois Lane would have done Superman, with no strings attached and without a second thought.

This is important, why? Let us do a quick comparison of what Lois thinks and knows:

Clark Kent
*Always around doing his job
*Never shows off his body
*Old school, Boy Scout
*Small town
*Clumsy, but lovable
*Son of Ma and Pa Kent
*Would go out with him if he asked

Superman
*Only there when she needs him
*Displays his legs, chest and package
*He is not old school or new school, he is in his on school, and he's a damn hero
*Different planet
*"The Man of Steel"
*Last son of Krypton, Son of Jor-El
*Probably thinks I'm stalking him

2 comparisons, 14 different responses… did you miss the fact that she is talking about the same guy? Learn this and learn it well: You are one person with at least 2 different personas just like Superman… the person you are and the person you need to be. The problem that most of us have, as men in committed relationships, is that we don't know how or forgot how to make the switch. Even worse, we try to be Superman at the wrong time or Clark Kent at the wrong time.

Elemental Factors

You could say that this is the metaphysical section, but it is helpful to get your mind in the game.

Focus now, to remember this later.

Earth: Body and brain
Your land (mind and body), your seed (children and stepchildren), your fruit (what you produce), your harvest (what you keep) are all connected. However, if the land is corrupted everything else is affected.

The Brain-Beauty connection. That which is good for your brain is also good for your body and appearance.

Make a list of 10 things that you know for a fact are bad for your body and brain that must be changed NOW.

Wind: how you sound and smell

How they talk on T.V.
Watch and listen to the actors on T.V. The criminals sound like criminals, the hero sounds like a hero, how are you coming across. Your tone must be confident, sure and clear. You must look her in the eyes, square on, when you talk to her and represent vocally what you mean internally. Look into the camera.

Your conversation
Ditto on "what" you are saying. Mind what you talk about in front of her. Ask yourself this question, "Am I really fixing the problem or making excuses". Even without their full conscience knowledge your women may be holding an article of resentment against you. It is not her fault; it is your own fault. It is usually a promise that you made that you haven't delivered on. It is something that came from your lips, which has coated her ears and has rested on her heart. Her heart is not heavy, but what she believed you would do, increases in weight when you shrug it off as trivial.

My brother's let me brutally ask you... are you showing up with the conversation of a small-dicked man? Impotent excuses, empty, blaming everyone else? You may be right and you may be telling the truth. But a big-dicked man starts off a conversation with, "Right now, I am going to... early tomorrow morning I am going to..." and he does it! He makes demands of himself and delegates everything else; he expects results and gets things done.

Your breath, your smell
This is very important because a woman's sense of smell is greater than that of a man. Don't take this for granted. Proper brushing, flossing and mouthwash are a small price to pay for something that may be secretly holding you back personally, as well as, professionally. Though she may or may not tell you this, even the smell of your feet can be a show stopper. Throw the shoes away with the most profound smell and get a pedicure.

Make a list of 10 things that you know for a fact, are real problems about the way you smell and that must be changed NOW.

Fire: your passion, vitality

My slant, if you will, about the things that you do and must do comes from a "fire-in-the-belly" perspective. Look at the thermogenesis of working out. You are burning calories, tearing down muscle, your temperature is rising your blood pressure rises, you are breathing harder... oxygen is a fuel. But no matter how good working out is for you, no matter how efficient your body becomes... the push to keep working out derives from a different kind of fuel; motivation, passion and sometimes just plain stubbornness. To be specific your mindset has to be: Your will be done.

Without passion you stand no chance of accomplishing anything, the winner is the guy who wanted it the most. Not the guy who wanted it the most on the day of the competition. It is the guy who has fought himself through the days, weeks and months of preparation and has defeated the opponent his mind several times already. This opponent is a force to be reckoned with.

Make a list of 10 things that you know for a fact need to be done for your KI (Killer Instinct) needs to be at its peak that need to be changed NOW.

One more thing: Early to bed to HAVE energy, Early to rise to USE energy.

The man the myth, little gods

My personal summation of thoughts about mythology and even the Apocryphal books of the Bible are that man is capable of many virtuous things. I do not believe that the different famous characters in history were much different than you or me. I do believe that these individuals utilized and mastered their God given talents and abilities.

Think about this: How did you feel when you were younger and watched a Bruce Lee or Chuck Norris movie?

Amped up? Psyched up? O.K. let's apply this to sports, admit it… even without a degree in physics… Michael Jordan made gravity his bitch? But how did you feel when you watched him? When I think of certain figures in mythology I get a charge that imbues me with a little spark that I didn't have before having the thought. How about you?

Mercury: Speed
Vulcan: Fire/Passion: cooking, artistic and talented
Apollo: War, protection
Cronus: Mastery of your time
Hercules: Strength, tasks/labors

What does marriage actually mean?

Marriage means quite a few things. Number one, it means that you and your spouse made a promise to be together, no matter what. It helps so much if your wife is your friend because your best friend wouldn't hurt you and you wouldn't hurt your best friend. Bear in mind that following my suggestions will make you extremely attractive to other women, as well as, your wife. That is O.K. Why would your woman want you... if no other women does? But always remember, part of being a real man is self-control and being able to say "No"!

A real man hates to utter the words "I made a mistake" and "It just happened". A real man knows that putting himself in certain positions will have bad consequences that he doesn't want to go through. That means "No Happy Endings", No HJs or BJs from co-workers, massage therapists, Facebook friends, old classmates, and ex's, etc. etc. etc.

R. Kelly sings a song where the lyrics state "When a man lies, he pierces the very soul of that woman." Listen to it! Because if you think she was cold before....

At home, everything may not be peaches and cream but that can be fixed, but when you sleep around and introduce the very real possibility of diseases, out-side children and disharmony into your house, you break things that cannot be fixed easily. You, as the man have access to a part of your marriage that no else has access to, it's fidelity. Fidelity is made up of 2 parts, yours and hers. The only way that it can be broken or tampered with is if you or your wife breaks it. Sometimes things get bad, but it is up to you to make things better. You are the head.

You set the tone for the success of your home. For example, if your house is not clean, you clean it or delegate someone to clean up. Do not let things which should be done be put on the back-burner. If you, as the man, do not set the standards who will? If you, as the head of household do not step up, your household will not reach its full potential, simply... because you did not try. You are the support for everyone in your house including yourself.

I am, indeed, a king, because I know how to rule myself. - Pietro Aretino

Matthew 12:29
King James Version (KJV)
29 Or else how can one enter into a strong man's house, and spoil his goods, except he first bind the strong man? And then he will spoil his house.

Mark 3:25-27
25 And if a house be divided against itself, that house cannot stand.
26 And if Satan rise up against himself, and be divided, he cannot stand, but hath an end.
27 No man can enter into a strong man's house, and spoil his goods, except he will first bind the strong man; and then he will spoil his house.

#2 - Upgrade and patch the operating system

After you upgrade the BIOS comes the operating system. In some cases it is Windows, iOS (Mac), Android, Linux, and UNIX. Etc.

This is the environment you work in and work with. The operating system works fine when you first get it, but over time it becomes inadequate.

You will outgrow it. There will be threats developed to affect it adversely. There will be flaws that will be found over time. Even with proper use it can become corrupted.

Bind the man, destroy the family

Knowing that it all depends on you is something that we get hit with from the media, from the pulpit, from our relatives… but who takes the time to help or enable a man to be a man, no one.

There are certain conversations between fathers and sons that do not happen. They don't happen because it never happened a generation ago or even a generation before that.

One gem of knowledge that I would wish to leave to my own son it would be this… if things are hard and complicated it is either because you are doing the wrong thing or you are doing the right thing, the wrong way. I have found that the simplicity of the formula (below) makes it easier to understand relationships. If you don't understand the relationship you will miss out.

*You miss out because you don't get what you need.
*You don't value it, until it is too late.
*You don't get what you should because the fruit in your hand can be eaten now.
*A moment's delight makes us forget that planting a seed comes before a harvest.

The formula is this:

Net result in a DESIRED area = (input + output) from a REQUIRED area

Spiritually = value what you receive from temple, church or mosque + giving charitably

Physically = value your nutrition in your diet + exertion potential enhanced through exercise
Mentally = value your learning intake + improvement in what you do, create and make

I, being born of the Christian faith, have that faith as part of my Basic Operating System. Through research, by the desire to seek knowledge, I learn about other religions and other faiths and my own faith develops enhanced meaning and more depth. I admire those whose faith is that of Islam because of their devotion and their adherence to prayer, fasting and charity. I admire the Buddhist because of their 4 Noble Truths and the Eightfold path.

The 4 Noble Truths:
 * The truth of suffering, life is suffering, everything is temporal, know thyself.
 * The truth of the cause of suffering, desire.
 * The truth of the end of suffering, end desire.
 * The truth of the path that frees us from suffering, The Eightfold path.

The Eightfold Path:
 * Right View
 * Right Intention
 * Right Speech
 * Right Action
 * Right Livelihood
 * Right Effort
 * Right Mindfulness
 * Right Concentration

The net result is that my belief structure is stronger because with the discipline of Islam and the structured simplicity of Buddhism, I do not have any questions of why things happen or what I should be doing. I can make decisions with more ease and clarity because I have zero personal conflicts about anything anymore. I am not bound if I am truly doing what I am supposed to be truly doing.

How do you bind the man? Better question, how are you systematically being bound in order to be a detriment and not an asset to your family?

- Being subtle, bind him without his knowledge.
- Stop a man from reading.
- Make him too tired to read.
- Negate his respect due to him. Respect is a result of the man leading, protecting and providing.
- Make him feel sorry for being a man.
- Eliminate his KI (Killer Instinct) and undermine his self-esteem and sexuality.
- Over-emphasize that women have a right to be critical of the man, but the man is to be supportive by being quiet and making her whims and short term goals the priority of the house.

Being subtle, bind him without his knowledge.

People can perish because of a lack of knowledge. A family can perish because of the lack of knowledge of the head of the household.

Look around and there are clear examples of this.

*The next "decent" paying job that you apply for may require a background check, driving history, financial history, drug test, credit report, employment history, education history, internet posting history and more. Not just your boss, but anyone with access can know more about you than you know about yourself. You will have to sign a document that will give your future employer unlimited and unrestricted access to your life history... if you want the job.

*Another example; one illness or unexpected death can wipe out the resources of an entire family for a generation because someone didn't take the time to get proper insurance.

Stop him from reading.
If the man of the house does not read then "not reading" becomes the norm in the household. Not reading means that you have not validated what you know and what you believe. Your knowledge is finite and will become obsolete. Your strength of what you believe will be weak unless supplemented and vetted. When was the last time you gave your children advisement and had a book or research to back you up?

Make him too tired to read.
I have to admit that it may be a little rough when you first start to make reading a priority but keep at it. 15 minutes a day turns into an hour very fast when you focus on what you want out of the material. You have to make time. You have to demand at least 8 hours of sleep a night and at least 3 – 4 hours of "me time" a week in order to reflect and think about what you have read. Your "me time" should be undisturbed and can be 30 minutes here and there or an hour at times. This is where you figure out what is the next step in using what you have read.

Negate his respect due to him.
Respect is a result of the man leading, protecting and providing. Even if you aren't 100% across the board with leading, protecting and providing... you are worthy of respect for that which you have done. People will try to negate your contribution but at the end of the day, if all you can say is, "I didn't walk away" then you stronger than most. In God's eyes you are great as much as you are responsible... you should be respected.

Make him feel sorry for being a man.
Some of the best and most liberating advice that I have received is, "make a decision, make a decision." and "Before they can say you failed, they have to say you tried." Yes, we get aggressive and yes, we get defensive... testosterone can do that. But when we bring our forces to bear, the more we have used and honed that raw strength that originates from our testes...

Empires can be built or empires can be destroyed. Cities can be built or cities can be destroyed.

Eliminate his KI (Killer Instinct) and undermine his self-esteem and sexuality.
There is a clear link between that something extra that kings, rich men, powerful men and even wise men have... their sexuality. Your KI (Killer Instinct) combined with what you are good at and enjoy doing are immensely powerful when you have a defined purpose and a clear vision of what you want. Sex is a residual manifestation of conquest.

You could not outdo Wilt Chamberlain, Bill Clinton, King Solomon or Tiger Woods in their arena, but in your arena, your lack of conquests could possibly be what is undermining your self-esteem and sexuality. You have to find a place to practice and unleash your KI (Killer Instinct). You need establish an arena to learn in, practice in and dominate in.

Over-emphasize that women have a right to be critical of the man, but the man is to be supportive by being quiet and making her whims and short term goals the priority of the house. If she has 10,000 dollar dreams, you will have 25,000 dollar nightmares. Instill in your household, "That we have to sacrifice, so that we don't have struggle." If you can take on another job do it, if not let her do it. But don't make concessions or agree without thinking about it, rationalizing and praying over it. After that, let your yea be yea and your nay be nay, decisively.

Scaling down, ramping up and the importance of Gordon Ramsey

One of the most profound periods of my life and learning was when I went on a binge watching Gordon Ramsey's "Kitchen Nightmares". The takeaway from this unorthodox education was that I realized:

PEOPLE ARE DELUSIONAL

If you take on the endeavor of watching the series, you will realize that people have the best intentions, will sacrifice everything, will believe wholeheartedly in what they are doing and will completely and utterly fail. They fail because of taking shortcuts. They fail because they don't want to hurt people's feelings. They fail because they do not delegate. They fail because they are the best person for crucial specific tasks, but they become encumbered with supporting tasks that they are not good at. They fail because the refuse to look at the facts.

- If something doesn't work, change or prepare to change.
- Don't overlook your local resources. You are seafood restaurant on a pier and you are buying frozen fish?
- Periodically, you need to rid yourself of at least 20% of your menu or your service offering. Let go of the extra stuff and focus on the remainder. It makes more sense to focus on being the best Pizza and Calzone joint, than a sub-par Italian Restaurant.
- Don't let people drag you down. Obliterate what you have to tolerate. You can deal with a problem person now or 5 years from now; if in doubt, let your financial ledger decide.

- Seek criticism, take in and analyze constructive and destructive criticism. THIS IS THE ONLY WAY THAT YOU WILL MEET AND EXCEED EXPECTATIONS.

Have you ever heard of someone who became very successful very fast but couldn't really tell you how they did it? If you investigate and research you will notice a very pronounced compliance factor running through the history of their success. You need to be examined in your capacity.

You must be appraised, verified, and checked for consistency, authenticity, validity...

WHY? Because this is the only way to not to be delusional.

You need to fail and be called on certain things in the early stages so that you can take a punch, use the force, control the matrix... Once you fail at something you have knowledge. We should always consider the knowledge obtained from failure as an asset or capital. It can be parlayed into wealth if you use it properly. This is the only way that you reach higher levels. It might be impossible to fix an engine on an airplane in mid-air; the difference is if you had to, would you? At its core, it is the results of tenacity to "do" not "try" to be evaluated and inspected. Over a period of time, this is how you show up with a knife to a gun fight, and still win.

Before you can retire rich, before you become part-owner, before having your own brand of shoes, before you are named the NBA's greatest player of all time, winning five regular season MVP awards, six NBA championships, six NBA finals MVP awards, three All-Star game MVP awards and a defensive player of the year award. Before winning the Naismith College Player of the Year award, before leading the Tarheels to the 1982 NCAA Championship, making the game winning shot. Before being named ACC Freshman of the Year, before the basketball scholarship from N. Carolina University. Before making the McDonald's All-American Team in High School. Over a period of time, you have to grow four inches over the length of a summer vacation and practice like a maniac, over a period time. Because at Laney High School you decided to try out for the varsity basketball team and you were too undersized and too inexperienced and got cut from the team and it hurt like pure hell. – Michael Jordan is the person referenced here.

Things you must master

As I referenced our collective youth earlier, think about if at age 18...

..What if you had the car that you have now? What about the place you live in? The job you have now? Even with the kids, the bills, the boss you have now? You have resources and knowledge that you didn't have when you were 18.

Your new goal is to revive the indestructible, cocky mofo that woke up every morning with a raging hard-on. How do you do that? Scale back on the B.S.!

Here is a fact for you: When you were 18 you were not entertained. You were the entertainment. If you didn't have more days when you thought you were the shit at around age 18 than you have now, I would call you a liar to your face.

In your late teens and early 20's you could take a girl out and spend less than $30 and it was very likely you were getting some. Flash forward to the present.. ..After paying bills, washing dishes, cooking, cleaning up, buying groceries and spending over $200 on a night out and you are begging for sex?

What changed? Simple answer, you.

What needs to change, simple answer again, you.

The secret isn't wishing for the universe to answer your wishes. The secret is to grab the universe by the balls and look it in the eyes and say, "I am going to improve myself by reading, studying, creating, working out and saving money… and you are going to either help me or stay the hell out of my way. I have better things to do than waste my time than waiting on you or her. I am tired of waiting!"

YOUR MASTER PLAN

In this day and age you need to have a "master plan". Why? Because what we are taught, told and believe is wishcraft. It is not logical and is not based on cold hard facts. All reports regarding the current financial crisis, job crisis, government crisis, healthcare crisis, real estate crisis, etc. should be a warning to you.

Imagine that when you put your key in your car and try to crank it and… nothing. Even if it does start after a few attempts… there is a solemn feeling in your gut that no matter what was on your mind before… this now has your total attention. It does matter what the problem is; battery dying, battery cable issue, alternator/starter going out, out of gas… you need to have a plan on how you are going to get where you need to go if your vehicle breaks down. You can fix the car later, if you can.

Take the preceding as a parable. You need to get where you need to go and you have received the warning that your current vehicle may not get you there. What do you do? Plan and have contingency plans to support the main plan. This is how you make a Master Life Plan.

If you have figured on retiring but have not saved for retirement then you will still have to work to survive. If you have not made provision for your children to go to college then there is a high likelihood… that they will not go to college. You have to take in account what you have, what you want and what you need to produce a desired result. It is your will. If your will is not done, it is because you confuse "wish" with "will". The words are spelled differently. They have different meanings. Only the important stuff gets done. If you get un-important stuff done, mostly stuff for other people, you only have enough resources to "wish" that your will manifests… it won't.

Wish-power is something they say in your children's Saturday morning cartoons.

Will-power is the gritty, "Get rich or die tryin-'" - I'm a testosterone fueled force of nature, type of thing.

Example:

I have…

I have myself, a wife and 2 children.

I want…
1. I want to make and save as much money as possible.
2. I want my wife to be self-sufficient to take care of our children, God-forbid, if something happens to me.
3. I want my children to go to college.

I need to…
1. I need to be more marketable in the workplace.
a. I need to upgrade my skillset, education and affiliation to that end.
b. I need to be prepared to relocate to get top dollar for the same amount of effort.
c. I need to monetize my hobby or interest to make it an income stream.
d. I need to adhere to saving regularly and control spending.
e. I need to invest and manage profitable investments.
f. I need to find and secure "rock solid" life insurance.

2. I need to evaluate my wife. What type of person is she? Is she independent and strong willed? Is she without real direction yet?
a. I need to help her find what she is good at and likes to do.
b. I need her to get motivated in order to get educated, then educated.
c. I need to be prepared to support her for a time while she is obtaining education.

3. I need to take a long look at myself and my wife, after deep reflection of our traits, habits and failures. With that knowledge in the fore front... determine "how do we" approach each child on an individual level.
a. I need to keep tabs on what my child is learning in school, every day. Also, to find little ways to supplement and reinforce what was taught.
b. I need to know what their weaknesses are and address them accordingly. Tutor, camp, specialized learning, etc.
c. I need to guide them into excelling into something that they are naturally good and something they love. I say trick because this is really an exercise in getting them to stick and stay on one thing long enough to master it. Only then can they move to something else. It needs to be something that they can have an audience for and can learn to hold their own in that particular arena.

Desired result...

THE MASTER PLAN

I will get a degree, training or skills related to my given profession and my side hustles. Work hard to become an authority in the subject matter, enough to teach it. Move to the most lucrative geographic location for employment. I will advertise and promote my side ventures and save the residuals.

My wife will obtain "portable" credentials so that wherever we move, she can set up shop and work.

I will insure that I have done everything possible to ease my children into an understanding of the basic process of learning, how to learn and have an increased capacity to learn. They will be able to teach themselves how to learn.

The greatest master plans take advantage of what you have, what you have learned to change and your sacrifices.

You increase your potential to make money or get resources. You do the same for your wife. Take your money and make it work hard for you. If you save few hundred to a few thousand dollars, life will be sweeter.

MONEY:

Cash alone can reduce your stress, make you feel better about yourself and makes you a more attractive mate. The Bible says that, "money answereth all things."

Attack your credit report because each decade that passes by, it is becoming more and more important. Right or wrong your credit report is being used to profile you. You could miss out on a great job because of your credit report. Your car insurance is impacted by your credit report. Fight everything on it, try to negotiate for pennies on the dollar but by any means necessary clean, clear and improve it.

TIME:

Cash management is the result of effective time management. If your job pays $13 an hour, could you find a job that pays $15 for doing the same thing within the same amount of time? If all appliances in your house (AC, TV, etc.) were turned off or unplugged while you went to the gym or bookstore would it lower your utility bills?

PERSONAL TIME:

AKA "Me Time"… Things like a twice a week spa nights, mandatory 8 hours of sleep and time for self-improvement are critical and crucial to your growth and well-being. Learning how to cook (save money and insure nutrition), clean (physical activity and stress reducer) or give a massage (reducing her stress) are like vitamins to you and your relationships.

Your best time speed cleaning

Living room_____
Bedroom_____
Kitchen_____
Bathroom_____
Whole house_____

Huh? You don't think that being able to speed clean your whole house is important? This is not just for her; you also need to be able to relax in your own home. If your wife has to clean the whole house that means less time for you know what. If she has to walk over clothes and clutter her stress level will be higher, translation, "no" you know what. Why would she want to get on the floor if it is never cleaned or vacuumed? You can quote me on this, "It is always easier to get a woman into a bed that has already been made." "Even easier with clean linen". Find out about Egyptian cotton and thread counts. (The higher the thread counts the better.)

REMEMBER:
BEING CLEAN ENABLES GETTING DIRTY!

Things that you need to change and work on

1 Things to stop: Excessive drinking, smoking and spending money without saving any.

2 Things to start: Working out, cleaning the house, staying groomed and spa nights.

3 Things to do; Dress better, learn to make money, learn to save money, have a daily agenda for accomplishments.

4 Preparing breakfast and dinner meals.

5 Step-up: She needs "Do Not Disturb" time for mommy.

6 If she normally does all the driving, you have to start doing it more.

7 Clean up and fix up your ride.

8 Know how to get stuff for free, not by stealing, by asking.

Simplify, Amplify, Exemplify

Simplify, when you have made the decision that enough is enough, you will realize the biggest hindrances are extra and unnecessary stuff. L, I, G it!! Let It Go!!! You can get 5 things done if you stop trying to do 10.

Amplify. I want you to understand something I call, "Sonic Aural Infusion". You can get energized by listening to music. What can happen is that you will notice with certain music your body and mind start to sync-up. For example, if I listen to Eminem's, "Till I collapse" or Ludicris' "Undisputed" I can out work and out-think most people. I have a soundtrack for studying. I have multiple soundtracks for when I go to the gym. I even have a soundtrack titled "Dolomite" for when I need to be in a focused, "true Boss" mode and get stuff done.

Exemplify. The truth of the matter is that it is input that goes into me, that I process as energy/fuel. From what I process, I produce output. Conversation and communication are the same. Don't take crap in. If you can't process it and you can't output it, it gets stuck in you.

Limitless – supplementation and limitations

Before I drop this knowledge on you it is essential that you understand cycling and adrenal fatigue. Cycling is the reason why people who just start bodybuilding get more results faster. Their virgin systems have to adjust. Your gains are the result of your body adjusting. Also, it is crucial to pay attention to adrenal fatigue. Overdosing on stimulants (Yellow jackets, red bull, caffeine, etc.) changes your physiology to the point that your recovery time is thrashed. You get maximum results from a virgin (clean) system. The more that you use stimulants, the closer you get to the point of diminishing returns.

There is a movie that came out a few years ago called "Limitless". It is really worth it for you to acquire this movie by any means necessary. The main summary of this movie is that a guy who wasn't really successful acquired a pill that gave him the ability to focus, concentrate and fully utilize his brain. However, he succeeded where others failed by realizing that he needed to sleep, eat and use his new found abilities to fine tune his life, the drug and minimize the side effects of the pill. To be honest we all have deficiencies of some sort.

- It can be not enough water
- It can be not enough food
- It can be not enough sleep
- It can be not enough exercise
- It can be not enough vitamins, minerals, etc.

Your emphasis on building a better version of "you" means more than taking supplements, working out, reading and planning. You have probably already done this with mixed results and spent a lot of money in the process. Your focus should be on using your past experience and knowledge to seek out the best supplements, workouts, reading materials and best plans to produce tangible results... that work for you.

There are also different systems and organs in your body that you must consider. The top level stuff is the topics they don't about on T.V., in magazines or talk shows. Research how to flush and detox your liver, kidneys and colon because when these go you are really screwed. Get and demand your own lab work to be done and see your doctor regularly. Make him/her work for you and don't take what they say as the gospel. Make him/her explain things well enough to you so that if you want to consult Dr. Google, you can. If there is a huge contradiction, get a professional second opinion.

Here is your homework: At stage 1 of any cancer is chemotherapy required?

Brain supplements

This brings us to the study of Nootropics. Because these are not regulated or tested like other medications, I strongly urge you to be careful when taking these supplements.

There are certain substances that can help you function better, feel better and work better but only if you are already working on being better (sleep, diet, exercise and reading).

- DO YOUR RESEARCH FIRST BEFORE BUYING THESE SUBSTANCES:
- DO YOU TAKE IT WITH FOOD? AT NIGHT HOW MUCH (DOSAGE) HOW OFTEN?
- KNOW WHAT ARE THE SIDE EFFECTS?
- KNOW WHICH ONES DON'T GO TOGETHER?

Workout supplements

NOTE: Tribilus affects your testosterone production, which affects your mood and aggressiveness.

WARNING: You must cycle Tribilus because even though it helps you the older you get or the more you need it, after 8 weeks YOU NEED TO STOP USING IT. Your body needs to produce the precursors on its own. THIS IS JUST A TEMPORARY BOOSTER.

This is where I have to use my consumer protection spiel: A LOT OF THE BODYBUILDING SUPPLEMENTS, SHAKES, ETC. ARE PURE, and OVER-PRICED CRAP WHICH YOU PROBABLY DON'T NEED ANYWAY.

The best thing I can tell you is that the following might be all you need for physical enhancement supplement:

*Tribulus – Testosterone booster (Cycle it! Not for long term use. (750mg at least once a day, preferably at night before bed)
*NO Explode (…or a stimulant) – pre-workout
*Any good tasting protein powder shake – post-workout
*Creatine Monohydrate
*I am not a strong proponent of multi-vitamins, but sure… why not.

Peter North supplement

I have included this because other than giving you a few inches, this takes less work:

Follow for at least 2 weeks:

- Water, pineapple juice, apple juice: as much as you can stand
- Celery every day. – 2-3 stalks are O.K.
- Horny Goat Weed (HGW) - (750mg at least once a day, preferably at night before bed)
- Tongkat Ali - Eurycoma longifolia
- MACA (pill form or powder with juice) 5 - 10GMs a day… (Example: AM 2gm, PM 4gm)

Workouts

The funny thing about you working out is that it does so much for you overall. Your general health, mental health and sexual health gets an enormous boost from just lifting weight for an hour, 3 times a week.

I want to you think about something while we are on this topic. The last time that you and your significant other had sex, did your arms shake while you were on top? She may not mention it to you but this can be a major distraction and also kill the mood. Her concern should be your stroke, not that you are having a stroke. So at bare minimum, you need to be able to properly support your body weight to even be ranked in the "lover category".

Two exercises that supersede any workout that I or anyone else could give you to be a "**Superior Lover**" are:

PUSH UPS: 3 X 20... JUST TRY
UNTIL YOU CAN DO IT!!!

SQUATS: 3 x 20... JUST TRY
UNTIL YOU CAN DO IT!!!

The other workouts I present here should be pretty quick but you must start with light poundage so that your body can adapt. **DO NOT PERFORM EVERY EXERCISE IN THE WORKOUT.** Even performing 4-5 exercises per body part is beneficial. If you work out at home, just do the exercises that you can do. In the gym, do not show off and try to bench press 200 pounds. If you work up from 10 pounds and 8 weeks later you are doing 50 pounds you are doing great. Your body has to adapt to get stronger. Also, when you lift weights you are tearing your muscles, tendons and ligaments down... the net result is that your body, given the proper nutrition, rest and exercise will compensate by rebuilding your body to accommodate what is happening.

Muscles grow on your rest days and when you sleep, not in the gym. Muscles burn fat and the process of working out puts you in a thermogenic "fire mode".

One more thing that I learned that makes a huge difference when it comes to getting the most results from lifting weights may seem insignificant. Do not grip the weights so tight.

I found an old workout book where the author advised that thumb over beats thumbs under. Maintaining your grip with your palm and four fingers may make you handle less weight, but it appears to isolate better.

3 day split

Workout 1 – Day 1

BACK

Exercise Sets x Reps
T-Bar Rows or underhand bent rows 3 x 8-12 "Pull to upper abs"
Wide-Grip Lat Pulldown 3 x 8-12
Bent-Over One-Arm Dumbbell Row 3 x 8-12 "Stretch at bottom, pull to side"
Seated Cable Rows *3 x 8-12 "Pull to upper abs"
Deadlifts 3 x 10-6
*Standing cable rows(pull to waist) 3 x 8-12
 ** Palm down forward, palm up back, left leg forwd with right hand.
Work up to the point where you can add one these, one workout at a time….
D Bar("V") to chest 3 x 10-15
D. Bell Shrugs 3 x 12-15
NARROW Reverse-Grip Pulldown 3 x 8-12
Behind Back B. Bell Shrugs 3 x 8-12

BICEPS

Exercise Sets x Reps
Cable Barbell curls 3 x 8, 8, 6
Standing Barbell Curl 3 x 8, 8, 6
Close Grip Preach Curl 3 x 8, 8, 6
Concentration Curl 2 x 10
Reverse curl 3 x 8-10

Workout 1 – Day 2

CHEST

Exercise Sets x Reps

Warm-up Pec Dec 3-4 x 10-15

Dumb Inc. Bench Press 4 x 8-12 "Feel the stretch"

Dumbbell inc. Flys 4 x 10-15

Hammer strength bench press 4 x 8-12

Dip (Lean fowrd, wide grip) 4 x 8-12 "Don't go to low, up is when you squeeze pecs"

Incline Bench Press 3 x 8-12 "Between clavi and nipples"

Decline Bench Press 3 x 8, 8, 6 "Between clavi and nipples"

{Squats 1 x 20

Strght-Arm Dumb Pullover 1 x 12-15}

SHOULDERS

Exercise Sets x Reps

Mini arm circles 4 x 8-12

Front raises 3 x 8-12

Arnold Press 3 x 8-12

Alt. Dumbbell Shrugs 2 x 10 (up and back)

Machine Shoulder Press 3 x 10 (arch back)

Dumb Upright Row 2 x 10

TRICEPS

Exercise Sets x Reps

One Arm tricep extension(lockout, barely brace each arm), Side then overhead

Tricep push down(lean in) or Close grip bench press

Tricep Kickbacks 4 x 12

Tricep Bench Dip 3 x 8

[FINISH WITH "SQUATS" 3 X 12-15

Workout 1 – Day 3

LEGS & ABS
NOTE: 5 minutes of light cardio beforehand to warm up knees.

WARM UP
Exercise Sets x Reps
Leg Extensions 2 x 15-20
Front squats(cross arms) 1 x 8-15

Exercise Sets x Reps
Front squats(cross arms) 1 x 8-15
Hack Squats 3 x 8-15
Leg Press (close4outer) 3 x 8-15 (after warm-up set)
Walking Lunges 3 x 10
Lying Hamstring curls x 3 x 10-15
Seated Hamstring curls 3 x 10-15
Stiff leg Deadlifts 3 x 6-12

or

Exercise Sets x Reps
Bodyweight Squat 3 x 20
Glute thrust 3 x 15
Leg Press 3 x 10-12 reps
Leg Extensions 3 x 12-15 reps
Stiff-Legged Barbell Deadlift: 3 x 10-12 reps
Lying Leg Curls: 3 x 20 reps
Seated Calf Raise: 3 x 15-20 reps
Standing Calf Raises: 3 sets to failure

ABs
Crunches 3 x until failure

Workout 2 – Day 1

BACK

Exercise Sets x Reps

Reverse Grip Pull down *3 x 8-10 Inc. (warmup 1 x 8-10)

Wide-Grip Lat Pulldown 3 x 8-10 Inc. (warmup 1 x 8-10)

One arm dumb row 3 x 8-10 Inc. (warmup 1 x 8-12)

Deadlifts 3 x 16-18 Inc. (warmup 1 x 20)

One arm shrug D. Bell 3 x 8-10 Inc. (warmup 1 x 8-12)

Behind Back B. Bell Shrugs 3 x 8-12

BICEPS

Exercise Sets x Reps

Hammer Grip Dumb curl 3 x 8-10 Inc. (warmup 1 x 15)

Preach Curl 3 x 8-12 Inc. (warmup 1 x 10-15)

EZ Bar Curl 3 x 8-10 Inc. (warmup 1 x 10)

Alt grip EZ Bar curl 3 x 8-10 Inc. (warmup 1 x 10)

Reverse curls(tennisball) 3 x 8-10 Inc. (warmup 1 x 10)Machine

Workout 2 – Day 2

CHEST

Exercise Sets x Reps
Dumbbell Flys 3 x 10-12
Pec Deck 3 x 10-12
Slight Inc. Bench Press 3 x 10-12
Decline Bench Press 3 x 8, 8, 6
{Squats 1 x 20
Strght-Arm Dumb Pullover 1 x 12-15}

SHOULDERS

Exercise Sets x Reps
Mini arm circles 4 x 12-15
Dumbbell Lateral Raise 2 x 10
Shoulder Press 4 x 8-12
*Dumb Upright Row 2 x 10
Dumbbell Shrugs 4 x 12-15
 **Hands above elbows

TRICEPS

Exercise Sets x Reps
Close Grip Bench press 4 x 12
One Arm tricep extension(lockout, barely brace each arm),
Side then overhead
4 x 10, 8, 8, 6 adding weight
Tricep Kickbacks 4 x 12
Rope push downs 3 x 8

[FINISH WITH "SQUATS" 3 X 12-15]

Workout 2 – Day 3

LEGS & ABS
NOTE: 5 minutes of light cardio beforehand to warm up knees.

Exercise Sets Reps
Squat 5 x 10, 8, 8, 6, 4
Leg Extension 3 x 12
Leg Curl 3 x 12
Glute thrust 3 x 15

CALVES
Exercise Sets Reps
Standing Calf Raise 4 x 12
Seated calf Raise 2 x 12

FOREARMS
Exercise Sets Reps
Forward curls 3-4 x 10-15
Behind back curls 3-4 x 10-15
Machine 3-4 x 10-15

ABs
Exercise Sets Reps
Planks 3-4 x 10-15
Leg raises 3-4 x 10-15
Lying 3-position knee raises 3-4 x 10-15

Workout 3 – Day 1

BACK

Exercise Sets x Reps
Bent-Over One-Arm Dumbbell Row *3 x 8
T-Bar Rows *1x12*, 1x10*, 1x8
Deadlifts *1x10*, 1x8*, 1x6
Wide-Grip Lat Pulldown 3 x 10
NARROW Reverse-Grip Pulldown 3 x 8
Behind Back B. Bell Shrugs *1x12*, 1x8, 1x8

BICEPS
Exercise Sets Reps
Cable Barbell curls 3 x 8, 8, 6
Standing Barbell Curl 3 x 8, 8, 6
Reverse curls 3 x 8-10 Inc. (warmup 1 x 10)Machine
Concentration Curl 2 x 10
Reverse curls 3 x 8-10 Inc. (warmup 1 x 10)

[FINISH WITH "SQUATS" 3 X 12-15]

Workout 3 – Day 2

CHEST
Exercise Sets x Reps
Bench Press 5 x 12-6
Dumb Inc. Bench Press 5 x 12-6
Dec. Bench Press 5 x 12-6
or *Dumb Neutral grip press
Cable cross over 5 x 8-10
* palms face each other

EXPANSION
{Squats 1 x 20
Straight-Arm Dumb Pullover 1 x 12-15}

SHOULDERS:
Use rest pause on last set, make weight amount go up on last sets…

Exercise Sets x Reps
Mini arm circles
Behind the head Bar Press 3 x 10 | HEAVY 4 x 12
Seated Dumb press 2 x 12 | HEAVY 3 x 10
Cable lateral raise 3 x 10 | HEAVY 4 x 12
"Overhead" lateral raises 2 x 12 | HEAVY 3 x 10

[FINISH WITH "SQUATS" 3 X 12-15]

Workout 3 – Day 3

Use one of the other Leg workouts but increase by 5-10 pounds.

Learn to make 3 new meals a month

They say the way to a man's heart is through his stomach. But women love good food. They like home cooked food, but they love it if someone else cooks it. For even more coochie credits clean up the kitchen afterwards.

Find out the foods she likes and learn how to make it at home. Find time to test recipes and perfect the meal, also cooking is good for your soul. Don't overlook the fact that with a little time, effort and groceries you have an excellent bargaining tool. Master the kitchen and you will lessen resistance in the bedroom. If you get resistance in the bedroom... shut down the kitchen... she can cook, I guess.

Learn how to cook good meals fast. I naturally gravitated to breakfast, even though I don't like eating breakfast. I started making vanilla French toast, peppered cheese grits, oatmeal, biscuit sandwiches and pancakes and got crazy good it. But listen to this, when I wanted to make a point about something and didn't make breakfast, the kids made it clear that mommy better make whatever concessions were needed... pronto. They fought, but I won. Long live the insurgency.

Learn how to use a crock-pot or slow-cooker to the point where you can start cooking before leaving work and the food is done before you get home. Master how to BBQ specific meats and vegetables as well. It's primal thing.

True story:

The weather was perfect in Miami so I decided to buy a Bar-B-Que grill and cook in my backyard one Saturday. I received a book called the BBQ Bible as a wedding present a few years before and I folded a few pages of some things that I wanted to try. After pre-lighting the coals and putting the pre-soaked mesquite wood chips on the coals and onions on the grill, my entire neighborhood knew by smelling, the god of fire was about to do his thing. Ribs and chicken marinated to perfection and BBQ basted skewered shrimp. Everything came out perfect and I even cleaned the grill afterwards. The following Saturday I did the same thing... but I heard a conversation over my fence that went like this,"

(Woman yelling): YOU AIN"T SHIT!!! ..I'M THE ONLY ONE WORKING AND I GOTTA' BUY THE GROCERIES AND COOK ALL THE DAMN TIME...AND TAKING CARE OF THE KIDS AND YOU DON'T DO SHIT! HE OUT THERE COOKING AND SPENDING TIME WITH HIS KIDS EVERY WEEKEND... YOU AIN'T NO DAMN MAN..."

I didn't hear anything else after that… but a door slam, but I will never forget that as long as I live.

Part of you being a domestic god is that you have to learn to cook, and then cook well. If she comes home and the house smells like you baked a cake, cheesecake or cookies and the kitchen is clean, you increase the odds of redeeming coochie credits.

#3 - Improve network/Internet connection

When it comes to using your computer to work with other computers, the strength of your network connection is paramount.

A brand new computer on a dial-up connection is going to be slow. An older computer with a Gigabit network card and a Gigabit connection is going to be faster... at least you may perceive it this way.

The truth is that the connection itself can be a bottleneck. You can be connected but the efficiency; throughput and service, have an effect on the experience of what gets done and how fast it gets done.

No matter how well you execute locally, your connectivity gives the ability to access resources, communicate with others and in a sense go places without leaving your location.

STACK YOUR PAPER

You need money! Why? Hypothetically, if you blow a week's pay on a vacation, any person could view that as irresponsible. However, if you save a few bucks here and there to save the equivalent of 2 weeks' salary, then saved separately for vacation, it would be an admirable and honorable act.

Let it sink in that you cannot put the cart in front of the horse. It is the reward of persistence and diligence long term vs. the looming sting of short term impulsiveness.

Using your talents, mind and body to make money and save money is a serious turn on to a majority of women, but notice... I did not say if you have money. The difference is your earning potential...

You are worth than the money that you have. You could pick-up and sell scrap metal, cardboard, pallets, cut a yard or two on the weekend. It adds up. But realize that you could have money leaks that can easily be resolved by:

- Cooking meals
- Quitting smoking
- Quitting Chronic/420
- Packing your lunch for work
- Riding with someone else instead of driving by yourself all of the time.
- Getting raises and bonuses.
- Unplugging appliances when not in use.

Meet your new crew

I have noticed a change in older men that you should be aware of. I call this "friend death syndrome." It is like this; have you noticed in the generation before ours what happens to the older guys when one of their friends dies? They change. Part of their crew is not there anymore. Even worse, from the outside you notice a change in their attitude, their personality and their swagger. It gets worse when year after year either their closest friends or brothers have life changing illnesses or just check out altogether. It takes its toll on you mentally because once you obsess on your mortality you will either start living or put your life on cruise control to the grave. Then the paralysis sets in when one day you realize, "I am the last one left".

I have found only one way to combat this. You have to make your children and/or step children your new crew.

Why them?
- They will keep you informed about the world.
- When you are 60, they will still have your back. Statistically, most of your male friends may be dead. …Just saying.
- As they see you, their truest best friend age, they face their own mortality and hopefully will make better life decisions. This will save you money in the long run.
- Your child's and stepchildren's knowledge, understanding and testimony of you… If you are Christian, Muslim, Jewish or Buddhist will be used for you or against you at your judgment. If you are an Atheist or Agnostic, no one should ever say anything better about you than your children.

- If what makes a country strong is a strong military (YOU) then your relationship with your best intelligence branch, investigative branch and special ops team (YOUR KIDS) has got to be STRONG! When you get feedback or delegate, I encourage you to consult with them.

Valuable advice: You job is NOT to keep them from failing or quitting. Your job is simply this: Do not let them quit or fail alone.

Next up... your in-laws

Love thy in-laws

I have quick question for you. If you had to have someone take care of your children or your car who could you trust? If your first answer is not your in-laws then you need to make improving your relationship with them a priority.

- Never betray them, even if they make a mistake and fail you.
- Help your wife mend fences with them. Some strife has been between them since childhood.
- Use diplomacy and tact to re-enforce family. Birthdays, holidays and family events should be encouraged and you should suck-it-up and participate.
- Realize that your nieces and nephew are more likely to have and appreciate a talent or profession that you have. You may be able to nurture them more easily than your own children.
- I say make them a priority and treat them a priority because in this life you never know who you will need and who is going to actually help you.

My relationship with my sister-in-laws and brother-in-laws is awesome.

I have had trips out of town for job interviews paid for, bills paid for, extra cash given to me, job leads, meals, borrowed cars, etc. because I had line of communication open with them before I needed something. Because they knew I was trying. Because I made it known that I value my relationship with them. Way before they were an option for me, they were a priority to me.

Work, Job and Career advice

One of my former co-workers, John C., told me story that you should commit to memory. It goes like this...

A man, who wanted a talking parrot, walked into a pet shop. He heard the normal sounds that you would expect in a pet shop. Cute little puppies were barking, kittens meowing and birds squawking. The shop owner looked up from behind the counter and greeted him. The man stated that he would like to buy a talking parrot and walked over to one of the cages. The owner said while pointing, "This parrot speaks English, over 500 words and has an Associate's degree. He's $500." The man looked puzzled and played along. "What about this one?" he motioned to a larger more regal looking bird. The other animals got a little louder. The shop owner tapped the metal cage slightly and replied, "This parrot speaks English, Spanish and French and has a Bachelor's degree, and I can let him go for $1300." The man started laughing and was cut off by a loud, deafening "SQUAAWWKK!!!" from the back room. The puppies, kittens, every animal in the shop was dead silent. The man slowly walked into the back room, to a larger sized cage that was covered with a white cover. He pointed to it and asked the owner, "Is that another parrot?" The owner said, "Yes, and I will sell him to you for $5,000." The man looked puzzled and asked, "I know why the other parrots cost so much, but what does that one do?" The shop owner leaned towards the man and answered, "I have no idea... but the other 2 parrots call him "Boss".

As I write this book some things have become painfully aware to me. The whole concept of a job has changed since my Mom and Dad were working. I will give you 10 things for consideration. What you do with this advice is up to you.

1 Never let 1 week or more of vacation time accumulate without taking it. Things are too unstable you may lose or have to fight for it.

2 If your supervisor doesn't cover for you, DO NOT COVER FOR THEM. G-Code.

3 Every month, as a mental exercise pretend that you are looking for another job. Find out requirements and salary to make sure you are in step with your industry. Don't be complacent; you are working with old technologies. Your replacement will be current and more valuable if the only thing you know is what your company uses now.

4 Staying on a job without training for more than 2 years will hurt you in the long run. Make connections and contacts and don't burn bridges.

5 Know your job from an industry perspective. What determines that you are the best at what you do?

6 Let superiors know that you know that if any promises or agreements are not in writing, you know it's not official.

7 The less people know about you, your family and personal business the better. You have been warned.

8 Assume that everybody at work looks at your website, blog, Facebook and Linked-In because they have nothing better to do.

9 Keep a journal, and if possible keep a backed-up copy of your emails ALWAYS.

10 If you are dumb enough you too can work for free and be on-call with no increase or flex time. If you are even dumber you can use marketable skills that you have outside of your job description and get behind on your work and get written up or a bad evaluation. Get paid separately, work separately. Be careful when working contractually for anything out of your job description because if something goes wrong, well... I think you get the point. But to be clear... *don't stay up for 3 weeks straight building the company a 7.2 Million dollar a year B2B web-portal... and one day it crashes... and you're still making $13 an hour.* Well, $13 an hour before the CEO demands that you be fired.

Oh, and keep a work journal.

UPDATE: Pre-unemployment and unemployment

Well, as life would have it but for your benefit... I was formally unemployed from 2011 to 2013. This particular section increases the value of this whole book. It deals with your survival and that of your family.

Pre-unemployment:

- Keep your bills where you can get to them.
- Keep your driver's license clean and up to date.
- Keep you and your family's personal identification where you can get to it. Birth certificates, paystubs, etc.
- Start establishing relationships with family members, friends, church family and your wife's family and friends. Relationships, where you can bless them or lend to them, while you have it. This is establishing a non-traditional line of credit.
- Update your resume on a weekly basis. This is always good advice but use your resume as a road map. Where have you been, where are you now and where are you going. Once a month do a job search based off of your current resume and demand of yourself for to focus on new topics, new subjects and new conversations that will lead to a better job.
- People you need to know and have on speed dial:

#1 A mechanic who knows you and knows your car.
#2 A notary
#3 An accountant, the one who does your taxes will do.
#4 A politician
*Your side-hustle, hobby or home business has got to mature, fast.

- If you have a mortgage: stay in contact with mortgage company and know what is going on at all times. Start structuring your bug-out plan. If you have to move or move in with relatives make sure you have established a relationship even if you are in flux.
- Visit a homeless shelter and donate. While you are there think about how would you make it in that environment. Even more important, how would your family survive in that environment?

Transportation

It is sometimes overlooked as a condition of your employment but without transportation, your job is in jeopardy. We have already seen in our life at least one government shutdown. Who can say that at a local level the same thing could not happen to mass transit, bus and rail? Late is late and no matter what the excuse and no matter how cool you are with your supervisor, time is being recorded. From my past experience, it was deduced that the time you logged into your computer minus 7 minutes was the time-stamp for non-hourly employees. Trust me on this, it is not hard to run a report to show who the top 10 late employees are.

Stuff happens. You know that and I know that so keep the following in mind.

- Check the threshold of your car alarm. Find out what actually will trigger your car alarm.
- Take a good look at your battery the day after it rains. Is it swollen, is there super corrosion? Ask your local auto part store associate for the best thing to put on the terminals AFTER you clean them thoroughly. The battery terminals themselves need to be good and tight. Make sure that the wires and terminal cables are firmly connected to the terminals.
- Get your oil changed and your tires rotated at the same time, Every 5,000 to 7,500 miles.
- Once a month have someone verify that all lights are working. Also monthly check your radiator, oil, brake fluid, power steering fluid. In some places you can even get a ticket if the little light for your license tag isn't working.

- Change your wiper blades every 6 months. Checking your spare tire and tire changing tools can also be done at this time. Easter and Thanksgiving will work. These are cheap compared to the wiper arms that can warp or break if you do not change the blades.
- Unless you are driving in the mountains or extreme traffic conditions, every four years change you tires and it get you brakes checked at the same time.
- When the brake light comes on or you hear that all familiar chirping, get your brakes checked. Demand to see the old brakes before the mechanic even touches your car.
- When it comes to security, we are taught how to think like a criminal. With this in mind I would not want to break into a clean car because, it is way too easy to leave finger prints and I would subconsciously think that I was being watched. However, a dirty car, millions of finger prints… O Joy, I peep what looks like your daughters IPad, your wife's new IPhone, is that a laptop carrying case? Is it empty or not? OMG, your son's Beats by Dre headphones, Wow, all of those cables… I could really use a cell phone charger… the bottom line is that in a junky car, your locks are more likely to be tried, your windows more likely to be smashed and it is a terrible way to start off the work day.

I trys to look out for my peeps. We are in this together.

Unemployment

1 As easy as it may be to chill out and consider this as a vacation, which you made need after the shock of not having a job… don't rest for more than 2 (two) weeks. There is something called, "the stench of the unemployed". It is a very real fact, the longer you stay unemployed the harder it will be for you to get hired.

2 Do not flush your 401(k) or retirement funds as a first resort.

3 Make sure that everyone who knows you know what you do and the specifics of your resume, first. Then, let them know that you are looking for work.

4 Get used to poppin' tags. When I was unemployed, for the first time in my life I had 4 business dress suits… all from the thrift store.

5 Start cutting costs immediately. You have time to analyze your bills and expenditures. My personal experience: When I was on EBT-Food stamps I discovered that I could get deodorant, dishwashing liquid, diapers, anything non-food, by spending over $50-$55 in groceries. The trick is that as a rewards member you get $5.00 off your purchase… that can be used for non-food items.

6 Be careful what you put on Facebook, twitter, etc. Don't flame.

7 Again, your side-hustle, hobby or home business has got to mature, fast.

8 While you have time off, clean up. Start throwing stuff away or donate it. Technically it's all clutter anyway.

9 Work on self-improvement. Get out of the house, get a cheap gym membership, get out of the house, stop smoking, get out of the house, go to a library or bookstore and of course, get out of the house…..

10 I know what some of you are saying. What about un-employment and food stamps (EBT/SNAP)? This where you need to sit back, relax and pay attention. Before you apply for assistance you need to know a few things:

a. You need to treat the submission of any application for assistance as the initiation of an investigation. They want to know everything about your household and what you don't tell them they will investigate anyway.
b. Every source of income you receive they will want to know about. When you apply for benefits make sure that you have made all of the money and saved all of the money you can, FIRST.
c. Your un-employment compensation can significantly affect the amount you receive in food stamps (EBT/SNAP) benefits.
d. You need to accumulate some bills to present as part of your paperwork when you apply.
e. When they say you need to be somewhere at a certain time you need to be there on time (i.e. case worker, career training, workforce, monitored job searches, etc. Be mentally prepared, these are very depressing environments).
f. If you go this route and depend on assistance, plan ahead to split your energy between satisfying their requirements and actually finding a job. They are not the same thing.

I know better than most how it feels for hard working people, people that have contributed and committed to a company to one day, not have a job. I also know the frustration of looking for employment, high and low, with all the hope and determination that you can muster and returning home questioning your efforts and your own self-worth.

Throughout my time of being unemployed, there are 2 things that I have discovered that I cannot do at the same time: be subtle and be honest. As a requirement of my commitment to insure the success of this book and to reach my intended audience, I am going to be Honest but I am NOT going to be subtle. I am going to meet you where some of you are now.

If this world is going to be a better place it is going to be because of people who have given their all, lost everything and learned from it. People, who have realized that they have to make decisions for themselves. …this is what I call Depression's Impression. We have one thing going for us that we did not have when we had a job: we are no longer delusional. We know things. We have developed capabilities and coping strategies. Our brains are re-wired to insure our survival on very little. While working, we accepted conformity… validating someone's perception that you cannot learn more and do more because, woe unto them… that meant that you are more.

Depression's impression is simply this, we have evolved. We have adapted and now possess that which is heritable, functional and in some cases, have increased in fitness. We now know the danger at sucking at the teats of our employer for too long. We have gained an ability that we would not have considered because they mere thought of self-reliance can be admittedly, scary.

However, Us, that have lost the comfort of a job have become battled hardened and we are **more capable, knowledgeable and more courageous** than THEM who kept their jobs during the recession,

As I write this next sentence, almost shaking, giddy with excitement, let me validate the last sentence of the last paragraph above with 2 very poignant questions.

Question number 1, Did you know that during the last recession there were more millionaires made than any other time in U.S History?

Question number 2, based on history who is more likely to become a millionaire, US or THEM?

Viable, lucrative options

Below are few ideas because it important to know when to go down in prayer, and when to get up and hustle.

Mr. Truck
How to make money the old fashioned way, with a truck.

Think fast. What is more valuable a car or a truck? Well, if you were going to purchase a vehicle and you are unemployed (Income Tax) a pick-up truck is the wisest choice.

Mr. Truck is not a mechanic, always remember that.

Mr. Truck is a force of nature.

- Most towing companies charge $60 plus additional for additional miles. Mr. Truck charges between $40-$50 for a tow.
- Mr. Truck charges between $10-15 for a jump if you need it.
- Mr. Truck charges a minimum of $35 to haul trash to the dump. $50-75 a load for contractors.
- Mr. Truck negotiates with contractors for pick-up and delivery of building materials and fixtures
- Mr. Truck charges $40 – $50 per trip for moving. To move you from your old house to a new house.
- Mr. Truck charges $25 to pick up your new large appliance and furniture from the store and deliver them safely to your house.
- Mr. Truck cleans his truck up weekly. Inside and out.

What you will need:

- Business Cards, the more the better.
- A tow rope and tow chains
- A standard tool box with tools:
- Jumper cables/Battery cables
- A Tarp
- Bungee cables and rope
- Blankets
- Of course, a pick-up truck.

Make money painting houses

This is about as simple as it gets. Drive or walk around and make someone an offer to paint their house. Leave a flyer or business card if they are not there.

- You need to be able to calculate how much primer and paint would be needed and price it for them. There should be an app for that.
- Avoid 2 story houses until you are really ready. They are a different beast.
- Be careful of houses with ornamental bars, on the doors and windows. This type of painting is very time-consuming and you have to be extra careful.
- Once you get a paint job, hire an experienced day laborer to help you and let them teach you the ins and outs of the craft.
- Ultimately, you want to form a crew. 2 Trimmers and 2 rollers.
- ALWAYS CLEAN UP.

Equipment needed:

- (Optional) Pressure cleaner or access to a pressure cleaner, you can charge a little more for this.
- (Optional) Patch holes and do some light surface work, you can charge a little more for this.
- 2 ladders
- Assorted brushes, according to the type of paint you are using.
- 4 Paint Rollers with poles/sticks
- Trash Bags
- Grills for 5 Gal. buckets
- Small buckets for trim paint

Cash Potential:

With a $400 job you can split that four ways at $100 a piece or, or, or paint 2 houses that day for $800 and still give the other 3 guys $100 and you get $700...

...2 days later follow up with customer and offer $150 – $200 to paint their driveway and walkway... this you will do by yourself.

Make money as a DJ

Most of our most memorable moments that we celebrate and cherish are accompanied by music. As viable way of making money this option should not be overlooked. Being the DJ means that it is your responsibility to create the atmosphere for a given event. Here are few events that you can "perform" at and build a business:

_____Differential / Regular / Primetime / _____

- Funeral wakes, Reunions, Birthday, Anniversary, Retirement parties: 4-5 hours   *$400 / 600 / **750

- School Dances: $700 / $900 / $1000

- Outside church events, Yard sales, Food stands: 4 hours $250 / $350 / Never

- Holiday parties: $700 / $800 / $1200

- Corporate events: Never / $1,000 / $1,850

- Wedding Receptions: 4-5 hours   500 / 750 / 1,200

Cash potential:

To make it worth your while financially you need to know 2 things when it comes down to charging, Differentials and Primetime.

- The Differentials. For Parties my sliding scale depends on: whether I know the hiring person (friend, family, church, etc.), I can pass out flyers and business cards, I get a plate of food (a good sized plate of food) and if the event is NOT during Primetime.

- Primetime, these are times when I will NOT do discounts, I am set-up no less than an hour before the event, and I charge more for events in Primetime. That would be Thur. and Fri. 7PM to Midnight, Saturday 6 PM to 1 AM and Sunday 5 to 12 Midnight.

Without oversimplifying things the only equipment that you need is:

- Playlists for different occasions. You can get new songs but for the record, most people have complimented me on my selection of songs that they loved and have forgotten about.
- A sound system with 2 speakers, sub-woofer(s), mixing board, I-Pod, microphone and cables.
- (Optional) …for corporate you MUST have at least 2 Wire-less microphones set-up and ready. They like clip-ons.
- (Optional) A generator, just in case.

Tips:

- **First**, get in contact with **Phil Morse**.

He is the MAN!

No one can get you up to speed to be a DJ and grow that business than him.

Go to http://www.digitaldjtips.com

- Know how long it takes you to set-up. Practice at home and test your set up often.
- When you first set up and perform your sound check, walk out to the street and use good judgment to make sure your sound is "tight" not just loud.
- Attend a few family events that have DJs. Watch, learn and ask questions of the DJ, but don't distract him from doing his job. If you hear party music at a park, around the block or anywhere else take a moment and get a free education.
- For corporate events you need to keep mind that they may not want you to be visible. They really just want your equipment and mics. Also have at least 2 good playlists with music that does not have words, background music really.
- Know exactly what the person hiring you wants. Be on time and ask questions.
- When working outside always be prepared for rain.
- Pay attention to what people like and what they don't. At a corporate event I had the normal background music playing, but when all of the speakers were finished… I played some reggae and reggaeton and the cougars went crazy. Women in the audience over 40 and 50 demanded that I got paid to play another hour.

- Nothing good has ever come from tracks with vulgarity and profanity at a social event. ALWAYS choose the clean versions of songs. When in doubt, don't.
- Tailor your playlist so that Grandma, Mom, and Granddaughter can listen and appreciate your music.
- Be prepared to lead the event if needed. Get people dancing, have games and honor different guests.
- Never underestimate the power of 30 minutes of Karaoke.

Unemployment Survival: Getting a job in the near future

OBJECTIVE: TO GET A JOB

ARSENAL OF WEAPONS

- Your 2-minute elevator pitch. Who are you and what do you do?
- Your Short form resume: Word (.doc or .docx), .pdf and .txt
- Your Long form resume: Word (.doc or .docx), .pdf and .txt
- Your pre-filled job application, hard copy and electronic copy
- Your reference list. Call them during the work week during work hours. Those who answer go to the top of the list.
- Your username and password list for various accounts
- Your "desire list": positions, salary, locations, and days/hours you would like off. (Personally, I would leave the Information and Technology career path for a 50-55k position to either write, demolish buildings or even bounty hunting.) :-)
- Your "G" List: Councilman, Mayor, 1 seated judge, Congressman, State official over Department Economic Opportunity, Governor and the President.

Before we get down to business, be aware that this has to be done over a couple of days and this has to be your sole priority to get the desired results. Your 2-minute elevator pitch should be similar to your cover letter and your resume should support both. Get a Linked-In and Facebook account, insure that both do not have anything embarrassing showing up. Get set-up on multiple job sites like indeed.com, careerbuilder.com, etc.

THE PLAN:

PART A – TARGET ACQUISITION

- Pick 10 companies that do exactly what you do
- Pick 10 companies that hire for your position
- Pick 10 companies totally blind
- Pick 10 government/county/state agencies
- Pick 10 people who are working and research their employers hiring process

It may seem as though you have 50 targets, but the reality is that there should be at least 100. Remember you have to find the competitors, the next organization/department level above your primary or an alternate to your initial targets.

Example:

- Pick 10 companies that do exactly what you do: An accountant could choose H&R Block, Jackson Hewitt... but shouldn't overlook ADP.
- Pick 10 companies that hire for your position: Using an accountant again... For every company with an accounting Dept. they normally have GL, AP, AR, line of credit.

- Pick 10 companies totally blind: Yes, even your kitchen table can be of assistance. Bread, there are at least 3 major companies that make bread within 3 miles of me. I recall seeing a warehouse with Nabisco on it, where was that again? Winn Dixie doesn't just have a store near, me there's a huge distribution center less than 2 miles from me. Oh crap, I used to catch the bus to an old job that was across the street from the Publix Distribution center! Where is the nearest Wal-Mart distribution Center?
- Pick 10 government/county/state agencies: If you live in Miami: Miami Gardens, Miami Lakes, North Miami Beach, Miami Springs, Doral, Hialeah, Virginia Gardens, etc. all have different administrative offices… that all do the same thing.
- Pick 10 people who are working and research their employers hiring process. They can give you info that can't be found on the Interweb or by phone, like who is the hiring manager?

PART B – INTELLIGENCE – Do not apply for any jobs yet! Your success depends on how much information you have and what you do with it.

JOBS POSTED BOARDS: Who is the hiring manager?
APPLICANT TRACKING PROCESS

PART C – ANALYSIS and DECISIONS

Who is their competition or overseer? Apply actions used in Part B to this group as well.

PART D – RECALIBRATE YOUR WEAPONRY

Modify everything in your "arsenal" to accommodate submission to targets in Part C first, then Part A. You use the job posting info and requirements from your competitor/alternate/higher-up agencies in "Part C" against the HR machinery of your primary targets "Part A".

PART E – EXECUTE – Now you will apply for jobs. Clear all distractions when you are posting. I, even I, have clicked submit and realized milliseconds later… I forgot to include references. Also, do not forget to include a cover letter.

Apply to postings under "Part C" first, and then posting under "Part A". The next day send notification or call to confirm receipt of submission. You need to initiate contact to get your application or resume pulled. At the very least they can be on the lookout for your submission.

PART F – JOURNAL

Journal all activity in relation to these job searches, interviews, responses or lack thereof. Also Journal all actions taken in Part G. Keep a Copy.

PART G – A.P.T. – ADVANCED PERSISTENT THREAT

This part of the plan is where stuff gets real. I understand that you may not want the exposure that is going to come from this next step. Maybe your lights are still on and your family still has food. But if your situation is near critical, if nothing else that you have tried has worked, and you have already tried everything else, you need to prepare to execute the "nuclear option".

I do not recommend that you take this option lightly because once you commit to this, THERE IS NO UNDO BUTTON. Your life will technically be open as public record.

- You send a copy of your 2 minute elevator pitch, your resume, your journal activities and indicate that you are looking for a job as per your "desire list"... to your "G" List: Councilman(AFTER YOU FIRST RUN OF PART E), Mayor(AFTER 2 WEEKS), 1 seated judge(AFTER 2 WEEKS), Congressman(AFTER 2 WEEKS), State official over Department Economic Opportunity/Unemployment(AFTER 2 WEEKS), Governor(AFTER 3 WEEKS) and the President (AFTER 1 MONTH). 6 Months in, if you have done everything outlined in Parts A – G, send a copy to Oprah or a celebrity, your local news team and 2 lawyers specializing in unemployment law.
- If worse comes to worse, consult with your attorney to insist that your journal be admissible in your defense.

#4 - Uninstall old programs and install new better programs

As many times that I have been asked why is a computer running slow, my first thought is, "How many different Anti-Virus programs are installed and running?" One, if it is outdated/expired is bad. Two is worse. Three... well, just imagine a fight between 3 people at one time.

If I had to say what I have done to make an immediate improvement to most systems it would be uninstalling old Anti-Virus and old unnecessary applications. The old programs worked well when you first got them but time marches on.

Do what you have always done and you will get what you have always got, but over time you will get less until you get nothing. It hampers your efforts when interfacing with others. It's time to produce results.

WOMD – Weapons of Mass Destruction

Changing the game by increasing the statistical probability of intimacy.

WARNING: Stuff happens that may block your efforts or blindside your best efforts... Don't get angry if something doesn't work. Always have a backup plan and never it make it seem like you are just doing this for sex. She will call you out on this one because, well, you are doing it for sex. My best maneuver when I was confronted at the end the end of a date night was to respond with, "I'm glad you had a good time, me too... I am going to go read a book and let you get some rest..." Within an hour she was begging me to come to bed to "talk".

1 Continuous Arousal

Any woman, specifically your woman, can be kept in a state of continuous arousal. Realize that you are dealing with emotions. A woman desires a man who other women would desire… Let that marinate in your subconscious. If your attention shifts and you start focusing on different things, productive things… she will notice and she will be curious. You lose a few pounds and other women notice. You display willpower and it will get noticed. You start talking about something you have read and researched, everyone will notice.

*Change your diet – Lose a few pounds.
*Work out – get buffed. Increase confidence and self-esteem.
*Drop bad habits – and work on becoming a better person.
*Favor reading over T.V. – You become more knowledgeable and interesting.

Think about it like this, when a company feels that it has to "compete" for your business the odds are that you will get better service, perks and extras. Economically, marriage is the ultimate business arrangement. But happens when either party becomes complacent because there is no competition? The same thing that happens in any business relationship: dissolution, termination and or outsourcing. The marriage equivalent being abandonment, divorce and or infidelity (cheating).

2 Pavlovian Response

Don't get the wrong impression about this. I am not saying to buy your wife. What I am saying is this… Even if you own your car, you still need to buy tires from time to time. You still need to pay for tune-ups and oil changes. They call this maintenance. And you still have to pay insurance.

I think this simple story says it best:

There was a man who traveled through hot, scorched farm lands and came upon an old deserted farmhouse. It was the hottest part of the day and he was parched and very, very thirsty. The man staggered around looking for water or shade and discovered an old rusty water pump. Next to the pump he saw a dusty old bottle with about a half-gallon of putrid looking water. "I am so thirsty but that water isn't clean enough or cold enough to drink. Besides there isn't that much anyway", he muttered to himself. The man decided to work the lever for the pump and nothing came out but dust and a metallic coughing sound. He tried in vain several times in the blistering sun and fell forward on his knees and reached for the old bottle of water. "To hell with it… ", he snapped in a raspy voice. Out of the corner his eye he noticed the glint of a small brass plate on the pump that read, "Use water in bottle to prime pump. FILL BOTTLE WHEN DONE!" A choice was made. The man poured about a quarter of the water from the bottle in the pump. He pulled the lever a few times and more dust came out, but the sound was different. It went from a chortled cough to a squeal. He poured half of the water from the bottle into the pump and no more dust came out, but the squeal got louder. But before he could utter his next curse word… There was a rumble. It was a scary type of rumble. It was the scary kind of rumble that made a man forget that he was thirsty. The man backed away from the pump, cautiously and concerned. And without any warning or notice, gallons upon gallons of fresh, cold water erupted from the nozzle on the end of the pump. Later he filled the bottle and took a rusty nail scratched on the little brass plate, on the pump, "It really works."

Lesson learned: You can prime the pump or settle for less.

Example: If you make her a sandwich or small meal after sex, instead of going to sleep, she will be more inclined to like intimacy.

3 Synergistic Arousal

She vibes off of your positive vibe. Why have for years, have affluent, well-educated women taken and still take trips to the islands and hook up with men from the islands? Yes, the taboo and freedom played a part, but ask the ones who have indulged. You will hear the same thing, "I loved his energy", "He had an easy going nature, he listened to me and made my complex problems seem minor and trivial" and "he made me so relaxed"

Don't overlook the fact that in regards to the physical descriptions that most women would list as a turn-on, "His Smile" is almost always in the Top 5. If a woman had a choice between a guy who complains about everything all the time and a guy who never complains... she would most likely choose the non-complainer. Why? Because the complainer becomes a magnet for negativity.

The trap starts off like this, she may start off a conversation complaining and you join in, complaining about other things. You may have started off listening, which is good. But you get sucked in and start talking about your problems and gripes. The end result: before you know it you have just made statements and affirmations that you do not have control over your life.

What woman wants that? A woman wants a man with desires, dreams, ambitions and goals. Anything less is an excuse. If you want to get it on, you have to have something going on. If you look good, feel good and take some personal time for self-improvement and reflection... you represent peace to her and not helplessness. Why do you always hear the reference about "the strong silent type" of man?

4 Intrigue

Intrigue is very attractive to a woman. Keep her guessing. NEVER plan an outing and ask her, "What do you want to do? Where do want to go?"

*Try out some restaurants by yourself. To take her to them at another time.
*Get up early on a weekend and get dressed to go to Starbuck's. Only when she asks, invite her.
*Work on your self-improvement in secret.
*Hide money for surprise trips and vacations.
*Learn to prepare certain dishes.
*Have a nice outfit that she has never seen.
*Get tickets to a movie show or concert that she would like to see.
ALWAYS REMEMBER: In every woman there is still a little girl that loves surprises

5 Stimulation

The cumulative effect of the way you look, smell, taste, sound and feel can evoke strong, overpowering memories of you. You can be burned into her memory forever if you make the effort.

1 Sound: If your deepest voice is in the morning, then call her on the way to work, use the Barry White effect. Make sure your tone is deep, but clear and do not hold a long conversation.
2 Smell: Put 1 (one) light spray of your cologne on your pillow or on a towel in the bathroom.
3 Feel: get rid of the rough stubble on your face and keep your lips moisturized and kissable.
4 Look: Get some comfortable boxers or seductively manly PJs and wear your jewelry until you go to bed.

You need to be a good looking, good smelling positive man who has his stuff together.

Since we are on the subject of stimulation, if the largest sex organ in the human body is the brain, what if we added the aphrodisiac of our own imagination? It is at this point that I must bring up role-play.

One part of of the "why" people go outside of their relationship is the excitement of something new and exciting. There is no spontaneity and too much of the same old routine. When people feel trapped, any form of stimulation can and may make them do things they wouldn't ordinarily do. Role-play allows a couple to explore within the safe confines of their relationship. It is far too easy for a man to overlook the power of a scenario for great sex, to just pressure his women for sub=par sex. I am going to give a few examples of scenarios that you can try. Feel free to improvise.

Scenario – Car broke down

Sometimes a stressor can be used as an interesting plot device in terms of fantasy and role play. Take for instance one of the most stressful things that can happen; your car breaking down. Almost everyone has experienced this and unless you are reading this roadside on your phone right now, we have safely made it home.

During the many times that it has happened to me I have often pondered, "How could this be better?" Extremely attractive female tow truck driver? Nope, big scruffy guy with indistinguishable tattoos and heaving butt cleavage exiting the tow truck killed that image real quick. LOL. So... I buy 1 Adult ticket to the theater of my mind and what I came up with is one of my favorites...

Car broke down:

   Male partner needs to be dressed up, suit and tie, new silk boxers, fresh haircut, clean shaven.
   Female partner as sexy as possible, lingerie.

You need to have a hotel room in advance close by. This can even work if you have one car. Get a nice room at a nice decent hotel, nothing scuzzy. This really works well if you both leave the house early in the morning and don't see each other for a few hours while you are both shopping and visiting the barber or salon. Try not to make contact, yet.

The male partner can actually check-in early at the hotel and prep the room: music, bottle o' wine, Alize, ice, more towels, lotion/oils, Lindt/Ghirardelli chocolates, subway sandwich (untoasted) / room service menu / or the phone number for pizza delivery.

Start here: Earlier in the day, the male partner sends a text with the address of somewhere safe near the hotel for her to break down. When she is ready, and let me repeat, when she is ready…

She sends a text: HELP!!! My car broke down.

He does not respond to the text but within 15 minutes arrives on the scene, this handsome stranger helping the damsel in distress. He then proceeds to seduce her by offering her a drink at his place and she eventually gives in. This part is crucial: she has to send a text to her husband to say that a really sexy guy stopped by to help her and that she is O.K.

Once at the hotel, the handsome stranger pours the drinks and excuses himself to the restroom, with his phone.

The jealousy dialogue: The male partner can either call her or text her as the "concerned husband" and question her about where she is and who she is with. Let the conversation build and get heated. Men: When you start feeling hot, amped up and your testosterone meter is blinking, "RAGE" "RAGE" "RAGE" hang up the phone, take few deep breathes and casually, calmly and with some swagger, walk out of the bathroom in mid-conversation and ask this sexy woman you just picked up, in your manliest voice, "Do you mind if I kiss you?" Channel ALL of the passion that you just had into one powerful, time-stopping, earth shattering kiss.

Why this works? This fantasy has all the excitement components of cheating without cheating. A booty-call or a one-night-stand within the confines of your marriage can be the most incredible and erotic experiences that you ever had, if you let go of your inhibitions. Add to that the fact that he is looking good and she is looking hot and his anticipation for her text. The jealously dialogue which alone can amplify a man's most primal urges and open the door for a woman's inner "bad girl" to come out and play.

Scenario – Bartender Evaluation

Bartender Interview: In this adult role play scenario, one of you is the person in charge of hiring a bartender for a friend's bachelor or bachelorette party.

Props: Liquor ingredients for the following drinks: Gin & Juice, Sex on the beach, a bottle of wine, and you can afford it, Tequila for Margarita, ice.

Interviewer sample dialogue:
What are your special drinks?
What kind on wine do recommend?

Bartender sample dialogue:
How wild will this party get?
What type of music will you have?
If I happen to be interested in a guest of the party can I ask them out? What if that guest is you?

When asked about the music, set the scene by playing some party music. Dance a little, then change the music to something romantic and let nature take its course....

Or...

The female partner drops 2 pieces of ice on the floor, displays full rear nudity display, and the male partner... helps her... Uh, find it. Yes, on the floor.

Why this works? This fantasy role play has the elements of dominance (for the interviewer) and submission (the bartender being interviewed) which can be adjusted to your comfort level. Also the added music and alcohol, for those who indulge, gives the atmosphere an intimate party type of atmosphere.

Scenario: News Reporter

There is a smart way to do anything. Take for instance nude photos. If you do it remember that something private can become public real fast. Do not include faces with body shots.

What about video? Well from my security background I can tell you that a good way to hide something is to hide it in plain sight. This brings us to our next juicy role play entry, the news reporter.

Props: a camera, a desk or table 2 chairs and a news script, sample shown below.

Wardrobe: The partner doing the newscast has to be professionally dressed like a real newscaster.

Scene 1: While the newscaster reads their script, the other partner acts as the camera operator, behind the camera. The camera operator then starts removing their clothes, one piece at a time behind the camera. Every time the newscaster makes mistake, the operator yells, "Cut" and the reporter has to start over reading script. When the camera operator is completely disrobed they sit down on a chair and put on a solo show, again, behind the camera.

Scene 2: The newscaster can start the script over but the camera operator sneaks under the desk. At first doing nothing, but starting slowly, does all manner of things under the desk to make their partner…. (I would say what, but it all depends you : -b

Sample script for news reporter role play:

===

107

Scientists have discovered a new body part. Recently a new ligament was found in the human knee which plays an important role for those who suffer from some knee injuries and continue to have 'bad knees'even after treatment.

Orthopedic surgeons Dr. Claes and Dr. Bellemans of the University Hospitals Leuven in Belgium have been conducting research for the last four years into looking into severe (ACL) injuries.

They have studied the knees of over 41 deceased cadavers using macroscopic dissection techniques to examine why some patients knees give way during intense physical activity and continue to suffer from what is called "pivot shift".

The types of tears are very frequent and common among athletes and those who engage in sports such as tennis, basketball and football. And speaking of sports:

In football the Buffalo Bills beat the Dolphins 40 to 6

Ravens over the Jets, 19 to 3
Steelers come from behind and beat the Browns, 27 to 11
Lions over the Buccs (Bucks), 24, 21
Cowboys over the Giants, believe or not same score, 24, 21

Tomorrow night: 49ers at the Redskins, game time 8:00 PM Eastern

In NCAA Football the big show, one game today:
Number 11 ranked Arizona State against Arizona, 58 over 21

…and how about that HEAT, All they do is win... Miami 132 over Orlando 99, they face Chicago on their home on Saturday.

PAUSE

Don't pack those Halloween costumes away just yet. Nobel Prize winner Dr. John Billingsly has discovered that married couples who routinely role-play live longer and healthier lives. 10 years of research have been conducted and proven that factors such as arousal, anticipation and stress relief release increases levels of good hormones and nerve chemicals that protect and enhance brain function, the immune system and heart muscle.

PAUSE

Law makers and the house and senate have agreed that Americans have had enough and what began as a simple apology, has turned into national fervor to win back the hearts of the people. As a result stock prices are soaring, tolls have been lifted on most major highways over the weekend, gas prices are at their lowest at $2.00 a gallon in most areas and the job market now has a surplus of 8% available jobs.

PAUSE

3 more bank executives have been convicted of mortgage fraud and misappropriation of government bailout funds. They have been sentenced to 30 years each with no chance of parole. According to federal investigators, there will be more arrests within the next few days.

PAUSE

START OVER

==

Why this works? Well, there is a riddle I once heard: What happens when an unstoppable force meets an immovable object? There is only one answer that I can think of... surrender. This role play scenario is a battle of wills but more than that, if done right, you can watch the tape over and over and no one will have a clue why you keep laughing. When done right, the kink factor can be pretty high because one partner has to be straight laced and professional for the camera and the other partner's objective is the polar-opposite, to tease, to tempt and to seduce. Also, we could all use some good news for a change. Am I right?

Scenario: Store Associate

Sometimes fantasy can use a hand from the real world. This role-play scenario gives you the thrill of flirting in public and a naughtiness component that helps you both stay in character. (Let us just say, hypothetically, I have 2 red polo shirts and a pair of khaki pants on the ready. I don't need to paint a "bulls-eye" on the store we did this at.) Just know that regardless of the store you just need to know the employee dress code. (I got one of those little blue vests too.)

Employee: The person playing the employee has to be dressed like an employee of the store you are picking them up from. Either of you can introduce yourselves first, you can flirt and seduce with wild abandon because, well, the "employee" goes on their lunch break soon. :-)

Store Guest: Take them out to a restaurant to eat for quick lunch. Throughout lunch fabricate and flirt. Work up to some kissing in the car. When you get home or to a hotel start undressing them as soon as the door is closed.

Why this works? You are adding exhibitionist components to your flirting and seduction. The real employees WILL be watching you. The other store guests will be watching you. Security will be watching you. There is also a bit of a power trip for the "employee" that can walk right out of the store and go have sex and the "Store Guest" getting mad props by just walking into the store and seducing a store employee.

(Note to self: Doesn't Home Depot sell those apron thingee's?)

Scenario: Construction Worker

This adult fantasy is almost always in the top 3 of most couples role play to act out.

Props: Hard hat, tool box, safety vest, new leather boots, add a ladder or step ladder.

Extra Topping: Actually fix something :-) , No seriously, actually fix something.

Lady of the house sample dialogue:

Hi, I got your number from a friend and I need some work done my house? What type? Some screwing, hammering and my pipes need cleaning out?

Construction worker sample dialogue:
Hi ma'am, I'm here to screw, hammer and clean your pipes out. If you have a problem with leaks I can lay some pipe, if that is what you need done.

Scenarios:

   Changing light bulb. She helps him steady a chair or ladder he is standing on and by mistake, loosens his belt.
   He is under the kitchen table to tighten some screws while she is on the phone, sitting at the table, legs open.
   She has to sit on the dryer or washer while it's running to make sure it's leveled properly.
   "Oh Snap, the lock on the bedroom door is jammed and we are stuck in here!"

Why this works? This fantasy expresses the stereotypical male traits of the ability to fix, tools, roughness, masculinity and strength. Looking and acting the part presents an extra dimension of maleness. There are times when women may love a suit and tie, but there are also times when she lusts for a roughneck. For men, being seduced at work, or for work, kind of changes our programming for the better.

TUTOR AND STUDENT

From my experience it appears to me that some of the best relationships that I have witnessed are either complimentary or based on compatibility.

Complimentary, for example, meaning that one partner is really good at making money and the other partner is good at managing the money. One partner may by the extroverted and can function with and is energized by large groups of people. The introverted partner loses energy and has to be shields-up to even be in the same party. But it is the introvert that dominates with one-to one conversations with people they have vetted and connect with.

Compatibility, is more of a "we are practically the same person" in terms of likes, interests and most subjects. Given the scenarios above. Both partners are great at making money. So great that they live lavishly and forget to pay bills, but it is non-issue. Even in the large-group party instance. Two extroverts can party every week and it is enjoyed by both even through their golden years. However, two introverts can get groceries on Friday and binge on Netflix for an entire weekend and be just as happy.

One thing often overlooked in relationships is the fact that each partner has learned certain things, has certain talents, even acquired knowledge through school or own their own. Through certain types of role-playing your mate can share and teach you things and who knows what can grow from combined interests. A husband in construction and a wife with mad decorating skills can create a home development empire in no time. A wife who is in cosmetology and a husband in the public eye can create an image and a brand to transform their lives. If I am I musician and I teach my wife to play enough to get a gig then we both benefit. What it takes is patience, a plan and encouragement.

TUTOR AND STUDENT

Make a list of subjects or topics that you can teach to your significant other if they are interested.
Resolve yourself that you will be patient and foster learning. This may be trip to the book store or a field trip even better take a class together.
I am going to repeat this later; you both have to act like strangers for your session. No partner talk, STAY IN YOUR ROLE.

=============================

Both dress the part as student and tutor. Tutor must have a study plan that is no longer than 30 minutes long. Include a small 5 question test and what you have taught and what they have learned.
I told you that I was going to repeat this later :-); you both have to act like strangers for your session. No partner talk, STAY IN YOUR ROLE.
Set a timer for 30 minutes when you start your session.
When the timer goes off, little by little, start seducing each other. Do it real slowly and subtly and build gradually. If you start your session in public, one of you seduces the other to go to "their" house. If your session is at home offer a massage to help them relax, turn down the lights, put on some music, offer a drink. You can also escalate from the point of the student needing to take a nap or the tutor needing to take a shower and the student getting the soap off of their back.

Sample subjects:

- How to pay bills on line.
- How to cook a specific dish.
- How to mix drinks.
- How to make a website.
- How to paint a room.
- How to play an instrument or sing.
- Who to wash a car.
- A history lesson about a specific event.
- How to write a business plan.

Extra Toppings:

Meet at Starbuck's, Denny's or IHOP for your session.

Why this works? After 30 minutes, hopefully, you both forget that this is even remotely sexual and you learn something and become interested. The seduction dynamic taboo of teacher/student role play is why this scenario is always in the top 3 (along with plumber/construction worker) for both men and women. You keep in character to enhance the aspect of the seduction dynamic over the dominance and submission aspects.

#5 - Defrag, tweak and modify performance settings

Once you have taken away the non-essential programs and have installed the essential programs, it's time to optimize and fine-tune. Opening, closing, deleting, moving and other stuff leaves fragments on your hard drive.

Over time your computer has to search an increasing area of locations to keep track of where parts of each file are located on a disk or disks. We must defragment to reduce hard drive search activities. Also your memory utilization affects running programs. We can upgrade the memory and can even change settings that that make better use of hard drive and memory working together.

Every cute thing your computer does uses resources. We modify performance settings on a computer so that importance/priority is given to the things that matter and turn off the things we don't need or even notice.

The Power of Sleep

Sleep refreshes and invigorates. It is what your body and brain needs to build and regenerate. On a personal note, I must confess that my own sleep habits were terrible. During the day I was dragging and moody because of it. This was an area of my life that made huge ripples across every area of my life. I was too tired to be productive. So when I made the decision to apply the same things that I am telling you to do in this book, I had to overcome this demon first.

My attack plan was 2 fold, find something to make me go to sleep deeply without side-effects and establish a good sleep pattern. First, I researched and found a product call "IChill". I take 5-7 ml. every few days by 8-9 PM. The second thing I did was to determine what would my waking and working hours would be. In my case, 6:00 AM every morning. Using the 8 hour minimum rule, I would have to be in bed (…and possibly sleep) by 10PM every night. When I applied this to Friday and Saturday night some great side-effects manifested.

When I get cranked up on Monday my body was used to it. The shock was minimized.

I found that sleeping in on Saturday means that I foolishly traded my reading time, my prep for the next work week (washing, car check, groceries, bill paying, cleaning the house, etc.); music practice and this caused me unnecessary stress.

I also found that sleeping in on Sunday means that I have traded waking hours and shortened my weekend.

"Sleeping in" was detrimental to my life and the quality of my life.

Before you go to sleep concentrate on the following:

For 10 minutes think about a mental list of 5 things that you must do tomorrow.
For 10 minutes think about a mental list of 5 things that you can do tomorrow.

Let your conscious mind dictate "What" but leave it to your sub-conscious to dwell and dream on "How".

#5 - Upgrade the interfaces: monitor, keyboard, mouse and speakers

Truthfully, you can hide the box/CPU of a computer and change the monitor, keyboard, mouse and speakers. If you have performed the upgrade path from steps #1 - #4, then perform step #5 you may be led to believe one thing... "I got a new freakin' computer!"

How you "interface" with the computer is a very intriguing aspect of an upgrade. If what you see is new (bigger better monitor), what you touch is new (wireless keyboard and ergonomic mouse) and what you hear is new (Volume control and OMG a sub-woofer) then 3 out 5 of your senses are registering... new.

Spa Days and Spa Nights

Women notice everything. They definitely notice when you enjoy pampering yourself and when you enjoy making yourself look better, it takes things to another level. These things allow your aura to grow and glow. On your spa days/nights try to get between 8-9 hours of sleep for the full effect. Personally, I think that Thursdays and Saturdays are the best because on Friday's most companies have casual Friday's or dress down day. Saturday's because if you are married you will probably be going out Saturday night. Plus, if you are going to church Sunday the spa night effect from Saturday should carry over all day on Sunday, even after church. Hint, hint.

Eat vegetables and fruits all day.

This is part of the brain – beauty connection. Strangely enough the same things that are great for your brain are also excellent for your hair, skin and nails. These foods may make you gassy but it's worth it.

#1 Acai – especially the pulp. Onions, garlic, chives, leeks, shallots, hulled barley, bean, buckwheat, fresh grass juice, Blue-Green Algae (BGA), Spirulina, Chlorella, chili peppers, sprouts, alfalfa, cabbage, clover, fenugreek, mustard, radish, sesame, sunflower seeds, adzuki beans, chickpeas, lentils, mung beans, green peas, wheat, rye, triticale, Pomegranate juice, salmon, blueberries, kiwi fruit, green tea

But no dairy, no fried food, no white sugar, nothing breaded.

SPA NIGHT!

- Work on your face. Is it oily or dry?
- Get a shave
- Make a light paste of Cetaphil and scrub your face lightly.
- Follow up with pore snapping... you alternate between using a hot towel and cold towel on your face for 2 minutes at a time. Doing this about 5 times each will minimize ingrown hairs and razor bumps
- Teeth Whitening, flossing and mouth wash
- Trim nasal hair
- Body: Cleansing bath: Concentrate on your neck, elbows, knees and hands.
- Hands and feet: manicure and pedicure (GO TO A PROFESSIONAL)

Colognes

Colognes are kind of tricky so be careful. Some fragrances work great in the summer and heat. Others are better for fall and winter.

While I do recommend using body washes, specifically body wash + shampoo (2-in-1), they could clash with your cologne. If you are depending on your cologne for your scent, use a less fragrant soap instead of body wash. Lever2000 may be all that you need.

- Rule #1 with colognes: ALWAYS WASH AND CLEAN BEHIND YOUR EARS!!!
- Rule #2: Before you spray: remember this mantra: For some fragrances 2 sprays is too much. You are not an air freshener, DO NOT OVER USE COLOGNE, JUST A WHIFF, and JUST A WHIFF.
- Rule #3: Don't be put off by the prices. Just by smaller sizes and samples.
- Rule #4: Cologne does not go on your clothes. They are supposed to mix with your natural pheromones to make it "Your Scent".
- Rule #5: Only apply 1 quick spray of cologne to your neck/chest, (one wrist may be good) wrists ... See rule number 1.

Bellagio: Daytime, Good for casual Friday
At first I didn't see what the big deal was about this cologne.
But years later I started noticing how many women's pupils
dilated whenever I wore this… it's a keeper.

Bvlgari Black (Bulgari), Daytime
This one is pretty good when wearing a sport coat and a little
bling. It completes the package. A little more complex than
regular colognes.

Envy Cologne (Gucci): Daytime
Good for a quickie lunch date with the wife.

Acqua di Gio, casual use
Seriously, wear this and your wife may get into an altercation
with other younger women trying to flirt with you.

Polo Blue, casual use
Very fresh. DO NOT WEAR THIS TO BED IF YOU PLAN
ON GOING TO WORK TOMORROW. Also, don't go
shopping alone when wearing this one either. You have been
warned.

Polo Blue, casual use… winter
More than a little on the "hot" side. By hot, I mean on the
cinnamon side. I save this for Winter and colder months. It
has notes which induce closeness. Polo is weird like that.

Tim McGraw's "Silver"
Clean and little heavy. Usually a good after shower or after
bath scent. This is my Nautica Blue replacement… notice I
said replacement, not substitute.

Dreamer, Versace
Kind of romantic, don't wear unless you have had a recent good haircut and shave. I personally wear this when I am in a melancholy type of mood. "I don't want to be bothered but if you want to get busy, be direct..." I am not in a mood for games when I wear this.

Bvlgari (Bulgari), evening use
It may just be my opinion but I don't consider this one for casual use at all. Suit and tie type of fragrance. The "Black" version smells nice, just haven't bought it yet.

Davidoff Silver Shadow Altitude –
In a word, "Clean". It lasted me about 4 hours which is good, because for the bedroom... this works. Women will remember this scent if they had a good time the last time you wore it. Women may follow you, again I say, it is very memorable. Body heat can reactivate this scent on you. Don't use too much.

Dior Fahrenheit –
I advise sampling different versions of Fahrenheit over a few minutes. I bought what I thought was a refill of the same Fahrenheit I already had and ended up throwing the second bottle away. Another note, oddly enough the shower gel is much better than the cologne. For Dior I think "Dior Homme Intense" is much, much, much better... HeWood by DSquared may be an adequate substitute.

Kenneth Cole Reaction
Consistently draws complements. It's good to keep this one handy because on quite a few days when I needed a confidence boost, I was wearing this.

Pure Havane – Thierry Mugler
Girls who smoke may be more drawn to you. Its higher notes
are cherry, honey and sweetish tobacco-like theme. Pure Malt
will get you more compliments though…

Versace Man, evening use
Do not wear this around older women. I call it catnip for
cougars.

Dolce & Gabbana, evening use
I always associate this with Starbuck's. I don't know why I
just do. ("D&G One" may be better…) stopped wearing it
for 2 reasons: #1 – I am guessing that a lot of women have
bought this fragrance for their guys birthdays, Christmas, etc.
I smell it everywhere. The bottom line is that too many guys
wear this already for my taste. #2 – I am really getting the
impression that this fragrance attracts men too. I feel the
same way about CK1.

Jean Paul Gaultier Le Male
IMHO it can be seductive but it smells "synthetic" and has a
very broad scent base. It is like an orchestra of scents. It has
even been described as "powdery". I recommend this if you
have had a recent haircut and shave. Your visual and scent
will match. It is like the shotgun of scents, may appeal to a
broader female audience than most colognes. Read this part
carefully: Keep in mind that it may appeal to a broader
female audience because it has feminine notes to it, and
because it has feminine notes you may smell attractive to
some men too.
1 SPRAY IS ENOUGH… it is strong and it lasts. Use very
and I mean very, lightly. Some may say you smell like mint
or apples or vanilla or cinnamon… this many different scents
remind me of only one thing… AXE.

PI, Evening use
Sweet-type of scent that I normally like when it's cold or if I am going out to the movies. Kind of like caramel corn… I want to wear this for Halloween to test a theory...

Egoiste Platinum, Evening use
I only wear this for going out. If you can find it, don't waste it on casual use.

AXE products
I like the Chocolate Sensation line "ONLY". Not the others, they kind seem like you are trying too hard, a little juvenile. Women who were hungry paid me more attention and kept conversations going longer. I could tell it was because of this by the almost uncontrollable movement of their nostrils and closeness.

Paul Sebastion in the black box - The Original
This is cologne that causes me to bring up the problem of body chemistry mismatch. BUY A SMALL BOTTLE OF THIS TO TEST FIRST. I borrowed this from my barber. On him it smelled pretty good, sort of "Pimp-ish" to me. I took a shower and put this on… immediately I had to take another shower and throw my drying towel in the washing machine. It did smell good but with my body chemistry I felt like discovered the "fountain of aging".

Paul Smith, Paul Smith London for Men
Coconutty and smokey, but worth the effort if you can find it. Some say this has an extra dimension and projects. I must highly recommend as an adequate substitute/improvement, Azzaro Chrome Legend. Note to self: "Check out Paul Smith Extreme, I heard it may be even better than London."

ODDLY POWERFUL:

Francesco Smalto pour Homme...
Georgio Red is secondary alternate, but by comparison Francesco Smalto is something from the fourth dimension or an alternate reality. I want to wear this with leather sooo badly. Knowing about this one cologne is worth the price of this e-book. I honestly did not want to include this one because of its effect on mortal women.

Leu D'Issey - Issey Miyake
Very fresh. Very good for warm weather. It is amazing but use responsibly. Personally, there are only two colognes that scare me. This is one of them. I am totally serious about this because of the very high probability that other women may call your woman to tell you to wear it again.

Geir Ness Geir Cologne
A sophisticated oriental scent, almost floral. By floral I don't mean floral like flowers, I mean guy-floral like ginger?

Musc Ravageur by Editions de Parfums Frederic Malle
S-E-X-Y.... First thing, this stuff can last 24 hours. Second thing, women can't find their panties in the morning when you wear this.

Lolita Lempicka L'eau Au Masculin Cologne
Crazy, Scary good. Sweet, like an anise rum gingerbread... after you have eaten licorice. It is extremely unique because it smells like a combo of your top 3-4 colognes.

Fluid Cologne By Iceberg
Smokey, cedarish and unique.

Oud Wood - Tom Ford
If you read what I said about Leu D'Issey being one of the colognes that scare me... this is the other one.

Rochas Man:
One of the most powerful scents that I've seen that makes younger women's pupils dilate.

Paris Hilton
If Paris Hilton was put on this earth for one thing, it would be to create this cologne. I can be in crowd with other guys wearing more expensive cologne and I would be sought out to tell everyone what I was wearing.

Hanae Mori
This cologne may have women start referring to you as "the guy who smells good".

Lanvin L'Homme
If you can only purchase one expensive cologne this is your must have, inexpensive back-up cologne.

Odeur 71 Cologne by Des Garcons (This an Anti-cologne)
Comme Des Garcons (1) Cologne
Comme Des Garçons 2 Cologne

EXPENSIVE, BUT IF YOU CAN GET IT, GET IT:

Creed" Green Irish Tweed: Your wife does not want you to wear this to her family reunion… ever. And don't even think about wearing Creed Aventus around her girlfriends. They will classify you as a "gateway drug". Ditto for Silver Mountain Water and Original Vetiver and Original Santal.

The power of one: THE ALPHA MALE

Technically, when your break it down the whole man-woman thing is based on dominance. In the past dominance meant that you would kill any competition. You can't do that anymore. In this day and age you must find different ways to stand out as dominate in her eyes. This begins with you as a man, being a dominant man. A dominant man always has a plan... a Plan B and a Plan C.

Confidence, confidence, confidence = dominance, dominance, dominance

The easiest way to have confidence is preparation. For instance, I can take my woman to particular restaurant because:

- I know the chef and I call him "chef" even though he may only be a cook.
- I know the worst time to go to a restaurant based on experience.
- I treat the people who work at the restaurant with respect and it is returned.
- Also, I very rarely go to the beach alone with my wife unless I reserved a room in a decent hotel on the beach.
- I call places in advance (sometimes weeks to save up) to know how much money I need to have before I go there. Even for parking.
- I keep an MP3 player on me with a dual-jack and headphones so both of us can listen to music to set the mood.

#6 Enhance the user experience.

Now with everything that we have discussed this far you should realize that if you have followed what I have outlined in the text, you are way too busy to be stressed about sex. What should be happening is that she has to compete for your time, attention and affection. You move into the realm of the manly-man. This is the result of the process. It is loud without making a sound. Clear, without any explanation needed. In the realm of the manly-man, you get what you want, how you want it or don't waste your time. Although men are the primary target audience for the Husband 2.0 culture, our goal is to achieve better, happier and more enjoyable relationships. I admit that I can be a little gruff with men and they get it. No problem there.

Our focus is to improve the man for the purpose of improving a relationship. However, there would be a serious flaw in my logic if I give great advice, as well as, thought provoking suggestions and the men-folks execute it flawlessly, and then I completely ignore the fact that there is another party involved.

HER

Before we discuss anything else about her, I need to make this one statement several times.

DO NOT BE CONTROLLING.

Most of the divorced women that I have consulted with, no matter how rich they were, no matter how attractive they were, have told me that more than infidelity, more the money and more than anything else there was one reason that their marriage failed...

Look at the pattern in over 20 different divorced women's past marriage, "He made the money and he paid all the bills, and I had my own money... but He was too controlling" I have heard this same exact statement, word for word since I have been a man. Whatever you have read before, whatever you read hereafter, DO NOT FORGET THIS...

moving on...

2 things you must be aware of at all times:

She is never in the mood, because she is always tired. Quite a few women stop drinking water before going to bed. They do this to keep from having to go to the bathroom in the middle of the night. If she has a glass/bottle of water before bed, it is easier for her get wet and be aroused for sex.

The "Constant"

Understand that there is a constant in your relationship. Understand that this constant cannot be destroyed. This constant can only be destabilized and disrupted. The constant is: she does not want to have sex; she does not want to have sex with you. As I alluded to before, you cannot destroy this constant. The number 1 reason that she is not getting in the mood is because she is tired. The number 2 reason is because you need to improve. Viagra and those funny little pills at the gas station are useless if you do not deal with the constant.

Not dealing with the constant vs. Dealing with the constant

Not dealing with the constant

- Adding 2 inches to your penis…
- A hard-on that lasts for an hour…
- Giving her an orgasm…

… vs. Dealing with the constant

- a much needed foot rub.
- cleaning the house and doing laundry.
- taking the kids out in order to let her get rest.

What women actually want

1 A man who displays Initiative and Confidence.
2 A man that will do a little extra, for her.
3 A man with good sense of humor.
4 A man, who listens, pays attention and reciprocates understanding, not a solution.
5 A man who treats her as though she is the only woman in existence.
6 A man that honors commitments large and small and expresses a commitment to commitments.
7 A man that can enable his "Bad Boy" mode sometimes.
8 A man that has a plan for today, tomorrow, this weekend, this year and next year.
9 Gifts and surprises.
10 For her man to put his presence on "10". Be there when she needs you to be there.
11 For you to love her more than you want to make love to her.
12 A man who is creative and spontaneous.
13 A man that can show her that he would move heaven and earth, as well as, his schedule just for her.

Pre Coitus

Why is foreplay important? 2 reasons.

Number 1, if you like or love to have intercourse for the longest time possible, you will get complaints from your customer i.e. soreness and cuts. If you learn to enjoy foreplay, you can consider that as part of the actual act. Technically, it counts as making love. In your (man) mind it might seem like you did it for "10-15" minutes, but in her mind it was more like hours. The reason for this is perception.

*Men wrongfully, naturally gauge and judge the time of intimacy from the time we stick it in.
*Women actually start from the moment that you aroused, seduced and excited them.
O.K. here is the bombshell...

What if you never aroused, seduced or excited them but still had sex?

Think about this. Re-read the last 3 sentences until it sinks into your brain.

Number 2, for really good sex she has to be lubricated and in order for her to lubricated, she has to be aroused. This is another case where porn can make you stupid. I can't go any further without telling you from most of my encounters that most women hate KY Jelly, oil and any other lubricant that you have to buy, they prefer their own. If you go on drilling her for an hour and she is not aroused and or lubricated, you will encounter some resistance the next time you desire intimacy.

As far as a great lubricant and massage oil, allow me to introduce… coconut oil. The refined varieties do not have the smell or organic particles. Find out which ones she prefers but have fun during the selection. Olive oil works pretty good too.

Creating the conditions for intimacy

1.) A clean safe environment: Keep the area clean from your doorway to and through to your bedroom.

2.) Purpose: When you go out with your family or just your mate, have a purpose. Whether it be Learning, Relaxation, Culture, Communication, Entertainment or Formal, have a purpose.

3.) Memory: Pictures, people, music, etc. create very strong memories when recalled.

4.) 5 Senses Stimulation: Sight, taste, smell, hearing and touch can stimulate hormones like endorphins and dopamine.

5.) You, outfitted, fresh, scented, speaking clearly and freshly shaved.

6.) Keep 3-5 "special" towels by the bed. Hint: She hates sleeping in the wet spot.

7.) Food: Main dish, Side dishes, dessert and a clean kitchen.

8.) Rest beforehand: 8+ hours of sleep at night is what you both need. Sleeping during the day does not help you.

9.) Comfortable temperature.

10.) Creativity & Plans. DATE NIGHT with the kids and without the kids.

Premature Ejaculation: Jamming .vs Creating a Masterpiece

Without getting too explicit, Making love and music are very, very similar. As a musician, I can tell you that there is a big difference between a jam session and actually performing a masterpiece. For one thing, if I am jut jamming I can play anything at any tempo and that is perfectly O.K. Jamming is supposed to be a self-absorbed, self-serving activity. I can funk as hard as I want, change tempo do what I ever I want to do. It is to relish and satisfy my desire to play what and how I want to. But when I have to perform, different story. I need to relate to my audience, engage and be sensitive to my listener. I learned a long time ago that it not good to just start "jamming", so to speak, when making love. It is far too easy to lose control. I believe that a majority of men don't realize yet that making great love is like performing a masterpiece.

Now to make sure that we all get this, repeat the following 5 words with me:

- Verse
- Pre-chorus
- Chorus
- Bridge
- Modulate Chorus

Sexual performance is just that, a performance. Penetration or intercourse is only just one part of the performance. It is just one section of the song.

I said it before; music and making love are very similar. Both require a tempo, a sense of rhythm and movement from the count off before the starting note to the last and final note.

140

Think about Beethoven's 5th Symphony. You know the one… "Dun, dun, dun, Dunnn." It was not his first Symphony; it wasn't his last one either. That one part that most people know is actually the first 8 notes of the notes of the piece. 3 notes the same and one different… followed by the same pattern a step a lower. It only lasts 6 seconds... The entire symphony lasts anywhere from 34 to 40 minutes and has 4 different parts.

Say it with me....

"Emotionally, whatever happens, I will keep the flow and the tempo of the masterpiece."

What does this have to do with you? Well, Beethoven was deaf when he wrote it but he still managed to create a masterpiece. Do you know that the first time that the most famous song in the world was played...The orchestra did not play it well, they only had one rehearsal before the concert—and at one point, following a mistake by one of the performers in one of the other songs for the program... Beethoven had to stop the music and start again. The auditorium itself was extremely cold and the audience was exhausted by the length of the program, 4 hours..., But did you know a year and a half later someone wrote the review? Not because it was bad, but because it took them that long to find the words to describe the experience.

Again say the following 5 words with me:

- Verse
- Pre-chorus
- Chorus
- Bridge
- Modulate Chorus

Just like when you are really making love, what makes the great part "great" is everything before and after the climaxes.

A great lover is a song writer and an artist performing at the same time. It is your engagement with your audience that is paramount, and where you can take them emotionally.

Say it with me....
"Emotionally, whatever happens, I will keep the flow and the tempo of the masterpiece."

Variations of verse establishing the context...
(Out of bed: small expressions to let your woman know what she means to you,
In bed: In-direct brushing and engage the senses of sight and smell), Establishing the tempo, never moving faster than the speed of your breath),

The buildup of the pre-chorus is a build-up of intensity
(Out of bed: Once every 1-2 days communicate passion without words... without sex, in bed: .an increase of intensity, move to engaging the senses of hearing and touch, direct touching, be subtle, BUT NOT AN INCREASE OF TEMPO!!!).

The chorus. The part that everyone has waited for, but once it starts it has to end...

(Out of bed: Do something specifically to make her happy without wanting anything in return Do not even mention it, don't take credit for it,

In bed: Pay attention to your audience of 1, enjoy her responses, Keeping the tempo, and making each beat count, making each note count, making each word count)... but it is not the end of the song.

How would music be if they only sang the chorus, if they only sang the hook? It would not make sense and you would never be able to relate to the song.

The bridge, a totally different portion of the song is neither the verse nor the chorus, but evokes a very powerful, totally different way to make a statement of the main idea of the song.
(Out of bed: Tell her that you want to focus on 1 small thing that you could change about yourself to make her happy you will try for a month,
In bed: The tempo stays the same but you are doing something different, switch to oral,) Same meaning, but a different perspective and or deeper revelation being presented. Even though the bridge might seem like a totally different song... It naturally leads right back to the chorus.

Be sure to observe that it is popular for the chorus to modulate to a higher key. (Out of bed: Have sex in the spooning position or standing up, in bed: A totally different sex position.)

The Basic Days

These are days that you must remember and surprise her on:

- Her Birthday
- Valentine's Day
- Your Anniversary

Why not Christmas? Because as stressful as the holidays are, you should be taking her out or sending her someplace nice to relax... Not buy more crap. I know it's hard to resist the urge, but do not go overboard for Christmas. You have been warned. Personally, I have had the most success with giving gifts and gift baskets out of the blue... success meaning she cried and the next morning I got breakfast or better in bed.

Gifts

Never underestimate the value of thought when it comes to gifts. The selection, the wrapping or bag, even the timing of when you get it to her is important. Always have some spots in mind to hide a gift with wrapping if possible. Here is a list of things that you can select as an excellent gift if you need to have something worth giving:

- Her high school yearbooks(s), if she lost it.
- A time machine: Get her an mp3 player with a playlist of songs from a year before she graduated high-school all the way through the year after she graduated. Do this for college too.
- A makeover followed up by a photo-shoot.
- A perfume that she would like to have, she may have mentioned it once.
- Something she picked up at a store and put it back. Go back the next day and get it.
- Full seasons DVD of a T.V. show that she likes. Maybe Soul Food, Grey's Anatomy, Zane's Sex chronicles, etc.
- A dress and a dinner date, then a concert or show followed by a night's stay at a good hotel.
- Jewelry over $200.
- Flowers sent to wherever she is for 2 days straight.
- Take her to get a girdle and bra.

Basket Making

Learning how to make gift baskets is a very good and easy way to give you wife/woman multiple gifts at once. It shows thoughts and creativity plus if you get good enough you can make some quick cash with your new skill too. I have divorced couple in my family and I asked the female partner "What has the best and most special gift that he ever gave you?", without any hesitation she stated, "…He took an empty coffee can, painted it, wrapped shiny copper wire around it and also made flowers and designs with the wire, it touched my soul, it was the most beautiful thing I had ever seen that was made just for me… and it was filled with quarters." I asked the man about this master work of passion and he almost fell over, said holding back a tear or two, "I made that over 30 years ago, you got to be kidding." He had to leave the room. Here are some content ideas:

- Gift cards
- Greeting Cards
- Jewelry
- Cash
- Alize, Egg Nog Vodka, Pre-mixed drinks
- Magazines about her interests
- MP3 Player with nice headphones
- Music CDs
- DVDs
- Inspirational books, Candy & chocolates (Lindt, Godiva, etc.)
- Baked Goods
- Perfume
- Nice picture in a nice frame
- Work order pad

Picnic Basket

Example:

- Cold drinks, stored by the chocolates to keep them cool.
- Bread (Croissants maybe)
- Dessert (pre-sliced, individualized) Cobbler, cheesecake, cookies-in-a-tin,
- Tupperware or food storage containers for Main Dish and 2 side dishes.
- Breakfast
- Eggs: Boiled, scrambled, fried or over hard
- Meat: Sausage/Patties, links, smoked, bacon, turkey bacon
- English muffins, croissants

Movies that you need to watch by yourself and why

Disappearing Act: This is what happens lose your focus, lose your way and blame everyone but yourself.

The Landlord: The position that you put your woman in when you refuse to grow up.

Daddy's Little Girls: The position that you put your kids in when you don't have a plan b and decide to let your family go on without you.

The Pursuit of Happiness: When your dreams fail, get better dreams. Persevere and endure and do not give up.

For Colored Girls Only: A not so gentle reminder on what happens when you don't get help or don't relate in a relationship.

Deliver Us From Eva: Being comfortable being your best self.

John Q: Consequences of an option…when all other options have been exhausted

Pay It Forward: A reminder about the importance of being charitable and that you need to contribute as part of your existence and happiness. Be able to say that you did your part.

I Got the Hook Up: Team building and trust against incredible odds.

Equilibrium: Team building and trust against incredible odds.

Good websites: Let your brain gorge

http://www.husbandbashing.com/

What I like about this site is it's anonymity and free open expression of what real women are experiencing. I also like this site because this is not women are saying, this is what they are screaming on the inside.

From the "About Us" page of the site:

- **What is HusbandBashing.com**
It's a place where you can come and vent, let it all out and feel good about it.
- **How does Husband Bashing work?**
Really? You really need a set of instruction on how to bash your husband? Maybe you are on the wrong site then, honey!
- **Who can use Husband Bashing?**
You, me, your friends, your family members, anyone. It's fun, it's rewarding and it's MUCH MUCH cheaper than therapy
Enjoy!
The Husband Bashing Team

I am strong believer in Paradoxical Therapy. Paradoxical Therapy is when you have a problem/phobia and in an effort to overcome it, you completely commit yourself to a controlled immersion of it. For an example, if you have a terrible fear of snakes you are put in the situation where you have to hold a snake, play with the snake and feed the snake. The next level, multiple snakes. You learn to overcome your anxiety and build coping skills.

Your mind has the ability to create very complex and elaborate negative associations to help you protect yourself. Your mind also has the ability to desensitize and diminish your perceptions. More common in men, the impact of their actions, the pain that they cause others, procrastination, lying, cheating, misplaced aggression, passive aggressiveness and one of the biggest, **taking our wives for granted...** are developed coping mechanisms that are being used to avoid and get through reality. We become delusional. We think that we can get away with treating our spouse as less than a person, because we have become delusional.

MEN:

This where paradoxical therapy can be employed once again. Even if you think that everything is fine in your relationship (See **delusional**, above), I implore you spend you to spend at least 20 minutes browsing through the posts on this site. Ask yourself if any this sounds familiar.

Another GREAT Site is:

http://christiannymphos.org and http://monogabliss.com/

Mission statement of the site:

"The mission of Christian Nymphos is to teach married women to walk in sexual freedom with their husbands, so they will be able to reach out and help free the women in their lives."

When I first visited this site on my phone a few years ago, I was surprised about the flow of the content and I learned from this site more than any other that to help people, you have to engage with people. The original creators *SpicyNutmeg, Cumingirl, Cinnamonsticks, and super contributors: GingerMama, Peppermintgirl and Sugar and Spice* really put in work to make this site successful. When I say *success, you really need to understand one of my definitions, hit counts: The site has been down since December 18, 2011 and it still gets more hits than most blogs and websites. Well over 26 million times the site has been accessed. 26,715,499 hits, the last time that I checked.*

But all is not lost. One of the founding members of ChristianNymphos.org, SpicyNutmeg created a blog called **Monogabliss**, http://monogabliss.com/

Monogabliss: *Monogamus, blissful, married sex as God intended it!*

When it comes to answering some of those deep, intimate questions from my female family members, readers of my posts and even the wives of men who have copies of my book, these are 2 of the sites I point them to.   Remember:

...Proverbs 14

New International Version (NIV)

14 The wise woman builds her house,
   but with her own hands the foolish one tears hers down.

More good websites

http://iUpgradeME.com
http://guymanningham.com/
http://zenhabits.net/
http://www.askmen.com
http://thoughtcatalog.com/
http://www.artofmanliness.com/
http://malexperience.com/
http://www.mensxp.com/
http://www.howtogetridofstuff.com/
http://www.justaguything.com/
http://www.primermagazine.com/
http://lifehacker.com/
http://www.lifehack.org/
http://goodmenproject.com/
http://www.neatorama.com
http://dappered.com/
http://verysmartbrothas.com/
http://www.dumblittleman.com/
http://brokeassstuart.com/
http://www.mademan.com/
http://www.stevepavlina.com/
http://www.43folders.com/
http://www.theminimalists.com/
http://www.dudepins.com/
http://www.menshealth.com/

Good bonding TV show series

You can get whole seasons on DVD or just get Netflix. These are a shared experience kind of thing. NO KIDS.

- **Spartacus**
- **Grey's Anatomy**
- **Prison Break**
- **Scandel**
- **American Horror Story**

If you lose, don't lose the lesson...

The title of this chapter is gleaned from the great comedian, Mr. David Chappelle, "If you lose, don't lose the lesson." ...As I stated in the begging of this text...

"My job is to give you your edge, your tools, your mindset and your plan to do 2 things:
#1 – To significantly reduce the some guy-running-through-your-wife probability.
#2 – To put you in a better position in case that probability in #1 is near or at 100%, to either forgive her completely or cash out and get and keep a much better woman."

If you have done everything that you can, prayed, worked through this text, prayed again and it's time to L.I.G. it!!! (LET IT GO) read the following before considering #2:

I heard this from one of the best speakers, preachers and religious teachers of our time, Pastor John Hagee, I paraphrase: There was a man who visited an Asylum for the Mentally Disturbed. As he went on his tour the head of the asylum. They walked past many rooms with people afflicted by various maladies of the mind. They walked to the door of a minimum secured room of a man who sat in a dark corner and just kept saying, in a low depressed, almost sighing tone, over and over, "Lu lu, Lulu…". It sounded like a dying bird, "Loo Looo". They continued on the tour. They took the elevator to the next highest floor and even before the elevator reached the floor, even before the doors opened, He heard the ungodly sound of a man screaming, "LULU!! LULU!!", when then doors opened they walked briskly to a door with just a small Plexiglas window. The man peered in and saw a man writhing in agony, ensconced in a tight fitting heavy

155

straight jacket, He hollered repeatedly, "LULU!!!"…
Running to get away, running in to the padded walls and
falling again and again. The head of the asylum looked at the
visiting man and said, "I know you may be confused and this
is the strangest case that I have ever encountered. The man
we saw downstairs was in love with this beautiful woman
named Lulu and she rejected him. This poor soul… is the
man who actually married Lulu."

Sometimes the best thing that God can do,
Is not answer our prayers.

Epilogue

What I know for sure... 7 things:

- Make God a priority in your life.
- Save your money.
- Don't live above your means.
- Take 10 minutes every day and shut everything off.
- Know your strengths and know your weaknesses.
- Take care of your body.
- You are not going to live in this body forever; you will take a last breath one day.

www.ingramcontent.com/pod-product-compliance
Lightning Source LLC
Chambersburg PA
CBHW061723020426
42331CB00006B/1068